REVISE AQA GCSE (9–1)
History
ELIZABETHAN ENGLAND, c1568–1603

REVISION
GUIDE AND WORKBOOK

Series Consultant: Harry Smith

Author: Brian Dowse

Also available to support your revision:

Revise GCSE Study Skills Guide   9781447967071

The **Revise GCSE Study Skills Guide** is full of tried-and-trusted hints and tips for how to learn more effectively. It gives you techniques to help you achieve your best – throughout your GCSE studies and beyond!

Revise GCSE Revision Planner   9781447967828

The **Revise GCSE Revision Planner** helps you to plan and organise your time, step-by-step, throughout your GCSE revision. Use this book and wall chart to mastermind your revision.

For the full range of Pearson revision titles across KS2, KS3, GCSE, Functional Skills, AS/A Level and BTEC visit:
www.pearsonschools.co.uk/revise

Contents

. . . .

A small bit of small print
AQA publishes Sample Assessment Material and the Specification on its website. This is the official content and this book should be used in conjunction with it. The questions and revision tasks in this book have been written to help you revise the skills you may need for your assessment. Remember: the real assessment may not look like this.

Elizabeth's background and character

Elizabeth became Queen of England in 1558. Many people at the time felt this meant she could not rule alone. However, Elizabeth had a number of strengths as a ruling monarch.

Elizabeth's family background

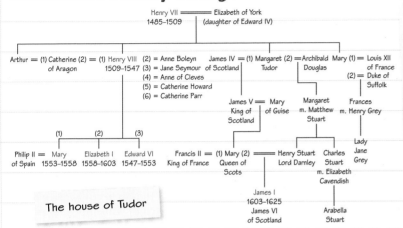

The house of Tudor

Elizabeth inherited the throne from her sister Mary. However, Elizabeth's position on the throne was insecure, as her mother – Anne Boleyn – had been executed for treason. Elizabeth was then declared illegitimate, so there were doubts about her right to rule. Also, Elizabeth was Protestant while many of her subjects, especially in the north of England, were Catholic. This meant Elizabeth had to be politically clever if she was going to survive.

Elizabeth's character and strengths

Elizabeth was confident and charismatic – this enabled her to win over her subjects and command support in Parliament.

Elizabeth was well educated – she spoke Latin, Greek, French and Italian.

Elizabeth was resilient – she had spent time in the Tower accused of treason and facing possible execution. She could cope with the pressures of being queen.

Elizabeth at her coronation

Elizabeth had an excellent grasp of politics – she understood the interests and ambitions of her subjects, and was able to use her powers of patronage effectively.

To find out more about patronage in Elizabeth's court, turn to page 2.

Although Elizabeth was Protestant, the number of Protestants in England was growing, making her position as queen more secure. She could claim Divine Right with growing confidence.

Reinventing the role

- Elizabeth used her strengths to re-invent herself as a different type of monarch. She liked to show that she was no ordinary woman. She argued that she could govern England on her own and did not need to marry.

- Throughout her reign Elizabeth portrayed herself as a strong, legitimate, popular monarch, who was married only to the country and not to a king. This is reflected in paintings such as the one above, showing a confident but feminine queen.

Key terms

Charismatic – possessing great personal appeal and able to win people over.

Legitimate ruler – someone who is legally and morally entitled to rule.

Divine Right – the idea that God alone appoints the monarch; so to challenge the monarch is to challenge God. Successful monarchs claimed Divine providence (Godly approval) of their actions, to strengthen their legitimacy.

Protestants – Christians who no longer accepted the pope's authority and many of the teachings of the Roman Catholic Church.

Now try this

Describe **two** advantages Elizabeth had when she became queen in 1558.

Court life

The court was one of the many institutions of Elizabethan government, which also included the Privy Council, Parliament, **Lord Lieutenants** and **Justices of the Peace** (JPs).

JPs and **Lord Lieutenants** were part of the local government, and ran different parts of England on behalf of the queen. The court, Privy Council and Parliament helped run the country as a whole.

The court – made up of noblemen who acted as the monarch's advisers and friends. They advised the queen and helped display her wealth and power. Members of the court could also be members of the Privy Council.

could be members of

The Privy Council – members of the nobility who helped govern the country. They monitored Parliament and JPs, and oversaw law and order and the security of the country.

Elizabeth I became Queen of England in 1558.

appointed

Justices of the Peace – large landowners, appointed by government, who kept law and order locally and heard court cases.

monitored and advised

Parliament – advised Elizabeth's government, made up of the House of Lords and the House of Commons.

The House of Lords was made up of noblemen and bishops.

The House of Commons was elected, though very few people could vote.

Parliament passed laws and approved taxes (**extraordinary taxation** – extra taxes required to pay for unexpected expenses, especially war).

appointed

Lord Lieutenants – noblemen, appointed by government, who governed English counties and raised the local **militia**.

Patronage was important in Elizabeth's court. This is where the monarch rewarded her supporters by granting them lands, jobs and titles. People who received these lands or positions could use them to become wealthy.

How the court worked

- Courtiers could use their presence at the court to try to influence the queen.
- The court involved up to 2000 people. Of these, many were employed as servants to protect and provide for the court.
- There was a strict dress code. Courtiers were expected to wear clothes made of gold and silver cloths and dyed velvet as well as ruffs, which expanded in size over the course of Elizabeth's reign. So attending court could be an expensive business.
- The court took care of Elizabeth's personal needs (food, accommodation, entertainment) and helped her govern.

Where the court met

- The court often met at one of Elizabeth's many palaces, such as the palaces at Greenwich and Hampton Court.
- Elizabeth's court moved around the country on Royal Progresses, staying at the houses of members of the nobility, who had to meet the expense of entertaining the queen and her courtiers. This included providing hospitality as well as gifts for the queen.
- Elizabeth was able to use the court to control her public image. For example, she used portraits to put across the image of herself as a woman in control of her court and her country.

Now try this

Explain **two** features of Elizabeth's court.

A **feature** is an aspect of a topic. In this case the topic is Elizabeth's court and an example of a feature would be the Privy Council.

Elizabeth's ministers

Elizabeth had a number of key advisors and ministers, including William Cecil (Lord Burghley), Robert Dudley (the Earl of Leicester) and Francis Walsingham.

William Cecil (Lord Burghley)

- Elizabeth's longest-serving minister/advisor.
- Became Secretary of State in 1558.
- Was created Lord Burghley in 1571.
- Also acted as Lord Treasurer, so was responsible for the government's money.
- Had considerable influence over Elizabeth and government policy, including:
  ○ the execution of Mary Queen of Scots in 1587
  ○ the war with Spain, leading to the defeat of the Spanish Armada in 1588.
- A passionate defender of Elizabeth's religious settlement, opposing Catholic or Puritan attempts to undermine it.

This 17th-century engraving of Elizabeth I shows William Cecil on the left and Francis Walsingham on the right.

Robert Dudley (Earl of Leicester)

- Ambitious and a close confidante of the queen, especially in the early years.
- Dudley received estates from the queen and became an influential figure on the Privy Council. This new power brought him into conflict with William Cecil.
- It was rumoured that Elizabeth and Dudley were lovers, a rumour reinforced by the unexplained death of Dudley's wife, Amy.
- Dudley's behaviour caused scandal, especially his affairs with Baroness Sheffield and Lettice Knollys, wife of Walter Devereux, the Earl of Essex. Both affairs resulted in children and led to him being banished from court.
- He was a strong supporter of Protestantism in England and the Spanish Netherlands, where he led military expeditions.

Francis Walsingham

- Member of Parliament (MP) for Lyme Regis before becoming the queen's private secretary in 1573.
- Closely involved in attending to the queen's security.
- Ran a network of spies, **agents provocateurs** and informers who uncovered plots against the queen, including the Babington and Throckmorton plots.

Agents provocateurs were people employed by Walsingham to encourage those who were against the queen to plot against her. This justified the later arrest and execution of the plotters.

Turn to page 23 for more on the Babington and Throckmorton plots.

- He used ciphers (codes) in all correspondence and developed ways of deciphering the codes of those who plotted against the queen.

Why were Elizabeth's ministers important?

✓ Elizabeth trusted her ministers and allowed them to shape government policy during her reign.

✓ Cecil and Walsingham had seats in Parliament and were able to monitor the opinions of those in the Commons and the Lords. They could persuade MPs to turn government policy into law.

✓ The desire to influence the queen led to rivalries at court, especially involving Robert Dudley and William Cecil and later between Robert Cecil and Robert Devereux, the Earl of Essex.

Turn to page 7 for more on the Earl of Essex.

Now try this

Study the image of Elizabeth, Cecil and Walsingham above, which was produced in the 17th century after Elizabeth's death. In what ways does it suggest that Cecil and Walsingham were important?

Relations with Parliament

Elizabeth needed to call Parliament if she wanted to pass laws and raise taxes. She sometimes faced opposition within Parliament to laws that she wished to pass or taxes that she needed to raise.

Why was Parliament important?

- Since the Middle Ages, the monarch could not raise new taxes – known as subsidies – on their own without consulting Parliament.
- Elizabeth's father, Henry VIII, established the principle of the King in Parliament. This meant any taxes and legislation demanded by the king had much better authority if approved by Parliament – the House of Commons and the House of Lords.
- MPs and members of the House of Lords could use Parliament to criticise the government and even the queen herself.
- Parliament could also act as a pressure group, for instance demanding during the 1560s and early 1570s that the queen resolve the succession issue by taking a husband.

The need to manage Parliament

- It was the job of privy councillors, many of whom held seats in Parliament, to persuade MPs and peers (members of the Lords) to pass the laws the queen required.
- By 1569 this was usually easier in the House of Lords, where many peers were bishops or courtiers. In the House of Commons, MPs needed to be persuaded using a mixture of threats and bribes.

For more on patronage see page 2.

- Privy councillors often sat on key parliamentary committees, to speed up the introduction of new laws. Elizabeth sometimes attended these committees, to help 'persuade' MPs to pass laws.
- The Crown could bribe and scare voters to try to influence who was elected to Parliament. This helped ensure that elected MPs were sympathetic to the government and the laws they wanted.

The succession: many MPs wanted Elizabeth to find a husband, give birth to an heir and so resolve the issue of who would inherit the throne after her death. A legitimate heir would reduce the possibility of civil war and foreign invasion.

Taxes or subsidies: how much Parliament should raise as taxes at the monarch's request.

Religion and the Church of England: the religious settlement of 1559, by which England became a Protestant country. It was also debated in Parliament in 1571 and 1587.

The poor: especially vagrants, who were seen as an increasing threat in Elizabethan society.

Issues discussed by Elizabeth's Parliaments

To find out more about laws that tackled poverty during Elizabeth's reign, turn to pages 13–14. For more on religious laws passed during Elizabeth's reign, turn to pages 19, 21–23 and 25.

Parliamentary rights: especially the right of MPs to criticise the government without fear of arrest.

The limits on Parliament's power

- Elizabeth did not call Parliament very often. She summoned 10 Parliaments between 1558 and 1603, which met for 140 weeks in total.
- Most MPs were men of business who wished to return to their estates, making them less likely to want to confront the government.
- Many MPs saw confronting the government as time-consuming and risky, and they could be punished for doing so. Indeed, Elizabeth could bully MPs who challenged her. For example, Peter Wentworth's determination to uphold the principle of freedom of speech led to him twice being locked in the Tower.

Elizabeth (top centre) before Parliament. The Lords are sitting and the MPs are standing.

Now try this

Study the image of Elizabeth before Parliament above, which was produced in the 17th century after Elizabeth's death. What does the image suggest about the relationship between the queen and Parliament?

Marriage and succession

The key problems faced by Elizabeth and her Parliament were that of her marriage and the **succession** (who would rule England after Elizabeth's death).

Why was the succession important?

- The key point of Elizabeth marrying was to produce a male heir. This would strengthen the monarchy by ensuring a male successor.

- Little was expected of female rulers in the 1500s, as it was unusual for a queen to govern alone. Unmarried women without an heir were seen as vulnerable and weak. A husband, who would govern on the queen's behalf, and a male successor, were therefore seen as vital to a female monarch's survival.

- If Elizabeth did not marry, there would be a disputed succession, as there was a wide range of possible successors. These included Mary Queen of Scots; her son James VI of Scotland; the descendants of Henry VII's sister Mary Tudor; Henry Hastings, Earl of Huntingdon (the Yorkist claimant); and the Infanta of Spain, Isabella Clara Eugenia. This could lead to civil war after Elizabeth died.

Why did Elizabeth never marry?

- Elizabeth was reluctant to marry, famously claiming in 1559 that she would be happy to have 'lived and died a virgin'.

- Elizabeth's marriage suitors included Robert Dudley; Philip II of Spain; Henry, Duke of Anjou; Eric of Sweden; and the Habsburg Emperor Charles IX. None was considered suitable.

- Philip II, Mary Tudor's former husband, proposed to Elizabeth early in her reign. Elizabeth declined; a Catholic king was unacceptable to strict Protestants and Puritans, who feared a return of Catholicism.

- Dudley was disliked by Elizabeth's courtiers.

- Marrying Charles IX, Henry, Duke of Anjou or Eric of Sweden could lead to military alliances and expensive wars.

- Any marriage would deepen divisions at court and lead to civil war. Elizabeth preferred to avoid this outcome by presenting herself as the Virgin Queen married to the nation.

Parliament and the marriage

- Many in Parliament were keen for the queen to marry, but did not want a Catholic suitor such as Philip II or Charles IX.

- By the 1570s the only remaining marriage candidate was Francis, Duke of Alençon, the King of France's brother. The Privy Council and Parliament were split on the issue:

  ○ Many Puritans opposed the idea of a Catholic being close to the throne, especially after the St Bartholomew's Day Massacre of 1572, when French Protestants (Huguenots) were killed.

  ○ Others saw the marriage as a way to strengthen the monarchy.

Parliamentary opposition undermined plans for Elizabeth to marry Francis, Duke of Alençon.

- By the 1590s, Elizabeth's authority had been strengthened by the defeat of the Armada, and Parliament had accepted the fact she would remain unmarried.

Parliament and the succession

- By the 1590s Parliament wanted clarity on a successor but Elizabeth refused to name one – to give in would reduce her authority.

- By the late 1590s, many assumed that James VI of Scotland, Mary Queen of Scots' son, would succeed Elizabeth – as he was a Protestant.

- However, Elizabeth did not formally name James as her successor. There were still many potential successors and to name James would have deepened rivalries and increased tension.

- James VI of Scotland therefore only became James I of England in 1603 on Elizabeth's death.

The succession was decided by the queen and Privy Council and not Parliament, showing the limits on Parliament's power.

Now try this

Explain why Elizabeth was reluctant to name an heir before her death in 1603. Give **two** reasons.

Elizabeth's authority in later years

By the 1590s, towards the end of her reign, Elizabeth was an ageing queen. She faced growing opposition within court and in the countryside, where bad harvests led to the risk of rebellion. Elizabeth remained a powerful monarch but there were signs she was losing authority.

Elizabeth's strengths at the end of her reign, 1590–1603

Essex's rebellion had been defeated, showing that Elizabeth was still in charge. Also, Essex's rebellion was directed not at the queen but at her advisors.

Elizabeth's authority was reinforced by military successes such as the expedition to Cadiz in June 1596.

Elizabeth remained in good health until relatively late in her reign.

The death of Mary Queen of Scots meant there were **no rival threats to Elizabeth's throne**.

As a result of the food shortages at the end of Elizabeth's reign, there was an uprising in Oxfordshire in 1596. In 1601 in Kent, a man was asked to attend court for saying, 'it will never be a merry world until the queen is dead'. This sense of unrest extended to Parliament, where calls of 'God save Your Majesty' were far less enthusiastic than before.

Turn to page 7 for more on Essex's rebellion of 1601. For more on the death of Mary Queen of Scots see page 28.

Elizabeth, painted at the end of her reign, in 1595, by Marcus Gheeraerts the Younger. It is one of a very few portraits that show signs of the queen's ageing.

Why was Elizabeth losing authority at the end of her reign?

Elizabeth was getting older, more bad-tempered and less clear in her judgement. The French ambassador, writing in 1602, described her as 'impatient', while she lost her temper in front of the Polish ambassador in 1597.

Her key advisors were dying. Francis Walsingham died in 1590, Francis Knollys in 1596 and William Cecil in 1598. This weakened her control of the court and Parliament.

There was growing infighting in court, especially involving 'new men' such as Robert Devereux (the Earl of Essex) and more established figures such as Robert Cecil (Lord Salisbury, son of William Burghley). These men fought for influence and the queen's favour (patronage), which weakened her government.

Courtiers began challenging Elizabeth's authority. The Earl of Essex nearly drew his sword on Elizabeth and had to be restrained by others from doing so. This led directly to Essex's rebellion.

Elizabeth was losing financial independence. She was forced to call Parliament in 1593 and again in 1601 to raise taxes. This weakened her position and exposed her to parliamentary demands about the succession.

Bad harvests in the 1590s led to food shortages and discontent, undermining Elizabeth's popularity and threatening rebellion. The situation was made worse by increased taxation to pay for a military expedition to Ireland in 1601 as well as falling wages.

For more on the system of patronage at court, see page 2. Turn to page 5 for details on parliamentary demands about the succession.

Now try this

Explain **two** ways in which Elizabeth's authority was weakened between 1590 and 1603.

Essex's rebellion, 1601

Essex's rebellion was led by Robert Devereux, Earl of Essex. It resulted from a weakened government and a difficult political situation towards the end of Elizabeth's reign.

Who was the Earl of Essex?

- Robert Devereux was a politically ambitious courtier, professional soldier and favourite of Queen Elizabeth.
- However, by 1598 he had fallen out of favour with the queen, after he distributed gold captured at Cadiz to his men rather than passing it on to the government. He had also failed to capture the gold on the Spanish treasure fleet crossing from South America to Spain.
- Essex was banished from court but was appointed Lord Lieutenant of Ireland and told to crush the Irish rebellion led by Hugh O'Neill, Earl of Tyrone. However, he failed to do so.

Robert Devereux, Earl of Essex. Note the size of the ruff around his neck as evidence of his status.

Elizabeth's power and authority were weakening. This led to more rivalries at court.

Rivalry between Robert Cecil and Essex. Both men competed for the queen's affections. By the late 1590s the court and the Privy Council were filled with Cecil's supporters. A rebellion would strengthen Essex's position.

Finance. Essex was not a wealthy man. His financial position depended on patronage from the Crown and was weakened when Elizabeth banished him from court and failed to renew his licence for the import of sweet wines. A successful rebellion would strengthen his finances.

Essex's ambition. Essex overestimated his support in both the court and the country.

Why did Essex's rebellion take place?

Humiliation. Elizabeth had slapped Essex in the face in 1598, telling him to 'go and be hanged', and he had to be prevented from drawing his sword in reply. He had also been banished from court. A successful rebellion would restore his status.

Military failure. Essex failed to put down a rebellion in Ireland, which led to accusations of treason. As a result, in 1600 a Special Court removed Essex from all Crown offices and placed him under house arrest. Rebellion was his only way to escape.

The rebellion, February 1601

> Essex gathered 300 of his supporters at Essex House, which he had fortified.

⬇

> The Lord Chancellor and other royal officers visited Essex, but he imprisoned them.

⬇

> Essex rode into London to gather support. This failed as the Mayor of London had told people to stay in their houses.

⬇

> He returned to Essex House, where he was arrested and sent to trial and the Tower.

Why did the rebellion fail?

- Essex overestimated his support. Many of the nobility, even those who sympathised with him, were not prepared to risk their positions and lives by challenging the queen.
- Government spies in Essex's camp, including Ferdinando Gorges, undermined the rebellion. For example, Gorges released Essex's prisoners so Essex had no hostages to negotiate over.

The consequences of the rebellion

- Support for Essex collapsed.
- Essex was found guilty of treason and executed.
- Cecil and his supporters dominated the court.

Now try this

Give **two** reasons why Essex's rebellion failed and explain each reason.

Living standards and fashions

Elizabethan society was very rigid and quality of life depended on social position. Those at the top of society were better off than those at the bottom.

The population of England grew from about 3 000 000 in 1530 to around 4 000 000 in 1600. London also grew rapidly during the 1500s, with a population of around 200 000 by 1603.

Social hierarchy: countryside

The nobility – major landowners; often lords, dukes and earls.

The gentry – owned smaller estates.

The yeoman farmers – owned a small amount of land.

Tenant farmers – rented land from the yeoman farmers and gentry.

The landless and labouring poor – people who did not own or rent land, and had to work or labour to provide for themselves and their families.

Homeless and vagrants – moved from place to place looking for work.

Ninety per cent of people lived in the country: less than 1 per cent were nobility or gentry; less than 10 per cent were farmers; about 90 per cent were landless, labouring poor, homeless and vagrants.

Social hierarchy: towns

Merchants – traders who were very wealthy.

Professionals – lawyers, doctors and clergymen.

Business owners – often highly skilled craftsmen, such as silversmiths, glovers (glove makers), carpenters or tailors.

Craftsmen – skilled employees, including apprentices.

Unskilled labourers and the unemployed – people who had no regular work and could not provide for themselves and their families.

Ten per cent of people lived in towns: 10 per cent of these were merchants, professionals and business owners; 90 per cent were craftsmen and the unemployed.

Obedience, care and conformity

- In Elizabethan society, you owed respect and obedience to those above you and had a duty of care to those below you.

- Landowners ran their estates according to these ideas, taking care of their tenants, especially during times of hardship.

- In households, the husband and father was head of the household. His wife, children and servants were expected to obey him.

People who broke the **Sumptuary Laws** could be fined, imprisoned or even executed. People had to conform to (obey) the rules.

Fashions

People's dress depended on social position.

The **Sumptuary Laws (1574)** stated that:

- only royalty could wear ermine

- only the nobility were allowed to wear silk, sable fur, and gold and silver fabrics

- only royalty, gentry and members of the nobility could wear the colour purple

- ordinary people including merchants, professionals and business owners had to wear wool, linen or sheepskin, and were restricted to certain colours.

Now try this

Write a short paragraph to explain why dress and fashion were important in Elizabethan society.

Prosperity and the gentry

Growing **prosperity** (wealth) and the rise of the gentry were key features of Elizabeth's reign.

Who were the gentry?

The gentry was made up of knights, esquires and gentlemen who lived in the countryside.

- ✓ 'Knight' was originally a military rank, but in Elizabethan times it became a mark of honour, with the title conferred (given) by the queen.
- ✓ Esquires, also known as 'squires', had knights as their ancestors.
- ✓ Gentlemen had become wealthy landowners by acquiring large amounts of property.

The gentry did not work with their hands for a living – they were not manual workers.

What was the 'rise of the gentry'?

- This phrase refers to how the gentry grew in size, wealth and influence in Elizabethan England.
- Some members of the gentry, such as Walter Raleigh, Francis Walsingham and Francis Drake, became more influential at court and in government. This meant the influence of many noble families at court declined.
- Other members of the gentry were able to join the nobility, whether through marriage, wealth or the willingness of the queen to give them a title (make them a Lord). For example, William Cecil became Lord Burghley in 1571.
- Many members of the gentry became increasingly wealthy. They could afford to build and extend houses in both the towns and the countryside.

Growing prosperity in Elizabethan England

The economy grew during Elizabeth's reign:

- There was growth in traditional industries such as wool as well as newer industries such as iron, tin and copper. These materials were exported, increasing the wealth of both merchants and the gentry.
- London, a city of 200000 people by 1603, grew in importance as a centre of finance and trade.
- **Privateering** brought in gold and silver stolen from Spanish treasure ships in the Atlantic.
- This prosperity boosted the wealth of the nobility, gentry and merchants, who increasingly owned houses in London.

Privateering was providing financial support for raids on Spanish ships and/or colonies, then splitting the profits.

- Professionals, including lawyers, also saw their incomes increase.

By 1603 a relatively small number of people in Elizabethan England (the nobility, gentry and merchants) had become extremely wealthy.

Montacute House in Somerset was built in about 1598 by Edward Phelips, an MP and member of the gentry, whose family had lived in the area for over 100 years.

A divided society

Not everyone was wealthy in Elizabethan England.

- Most people, especially the labouring classes, remained relatively poor and struggled to provide for themselves.
- During the 1590s bad harvests and rising prices, as well as falling wages, meant that many ordinary people (labourers) struggled to provide for their families.
- Others became vagrants, moving from place to place in search of work and often reduced to begging.

The wealthy, including members of the gentry, increasingly saw the poor as a threat to their prosperity. This was because, in times of hardship, the poor's involvement in riots and rebellions threatened the gentry's lives and property.

Turn to pages 12–14 for more on poverty during the Elizabethan period.

Now try this

List **three** reasons for the growth in prosperity in Elizabethan England.

The Elizabethan theatre

The theatre was an important source of entertainment in Elizabethan England, producing plays that were a mirror of their time, as they reflected the society in which they were performed.

Theatre design

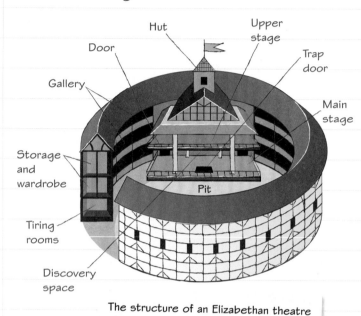

The structure of an Elizabethan theatre

Labels: Hut, Upper stage, Door, Trap door, Gallery, Main stage, Storage and wardrobe, Tiring rooms, Discovery space, Pit

The structure of an Elizabethan theatre reflected English society.

- Ordinary people or 'groundlings' watched the plays standing in a pit.
- Wealthier people sat in stadium-style seats around the stage.
- Members of the gentry and merchants sat in the galleries and on occasion on the stage, with plays performed around them.

Tiring rooms allowed actors to change into costumes for performances. Actors could also be lowered onto the stage from above using a system of wires and pulleys.

The theatre

- Mystery Plays, popular with many Catholics, were replaced with new, secular (non-religious) plays. These were shown in purpose-built theatres, such as the Red Lion, the Globe and the Rose.
- Comedies, performed by teams of professional players funded by wealthy noblemen, were very popular. Sponsors included the queen and the Earl of Leicester, and their performers were known as Queen's Men and Leicester's Men.
- All social classes attended the theatre, so purpose-built theatres had to be built to accommodate growing audiences.
- Elizabethan playwrights included William Shakespeare, Christopher Marlowe and Ben Jonson.
- Elizabethan actors were also important and included Richard Burbage.
- Examples of Elizabethan theatres included the Globe, the Bull Ring, the Newington Butts and the Bear Garden.

The importance of the Elizabethan theatre

Elizabethan plays reflected the society in which they were performed. For example:

- Marlowe's *Doctor Faustus* reflected the growing fascination with witchcraft that gripped some sections of Elizabethan society. For others the play represented the debate between Calvinists, who supported predestination (the idea that our lives are decided for us by God), and those who believed in free will.
- Plays reflected the vulgarity of many Elizabethans. The **bawdy jigs** performed in theatres such as the Globe referred to adulterous wives, milkmaids, prostitutes, thieves and muggers.

Bawdy jigs were songs and dances performed by Elizabethan players often wearing clown costumes. They usually contained rude words and actions, and sometimes the audience was encouraged to join in.

Now try this

Give **two** reasons why the theatre was important in Elizabethan times.

Attitudes to the theatre

Different social groups had different attitudes towards the theatre during Elizabeth's reign.

Why was the Elizabethan theatre so popular?

- It was a cheap form of entertainment – people could stand and watch plays for very little money.
- It appealed to all social classes. Even those who could not read and write could follow the performances, some of which were put on in inns and taverns. Purpose-built theatres designed by James Burbage contained galleries for members of the gentry and nobility.
- Plays appealed to people's different tastes, with history plays (for example, Shakespeare's *Richard III* and Marlowe's *Edward II*), comedies (for example, Middleton's *A Chaste Maid in Cheapside*) and tragedies (for example, Marlowe's *Doctor Faustus*).
- Elizabeth I enjoyed acting, and encouraged the development of acting and theatre at court and elsewhere.

An Elizabethan theatre used as a bear pit. Theatres doubled up as bear pits, brothels and gambling houses, allowing them to cater for a range of interests and tastes.

The queen – Elizabeth I never attended the theatre but enjoyed watching plays at court and funded a group of actors.

The nobility – could get seats on the stage itself, allowing them to show off their clothes, wealth and prestige. They often funded teams of actors, adding to the nobility's sense of importance.

Elizabethan social groups and why they enjoyed going to the theatre

The gentry and merchants – could buy **boxes** in the theatre, where they could entertain their friends and business partners.

The poor – could gain cheap admission, allowing them to stand close to the stage. This is why they were known as 'groundlings'.

A theatre **box** is a small separate seating area with a good view of the stage, for a limited number of people (usually around 3 to 5).

Negative attitudes towards the theatre

Many **Puritans** disliked the theatre, arguing:

- it encouraged bawdy, drunken behaviour as well as sinful habits such as prostitution
- many of the players were disreputable
- many plays contained immoral references to sex, drunkenness and witchcraft.

Puritan distaste for the theatre was especially strong among the merchant classes in London.

Turn to page 24 for more on the Puritans.

Theatres often attracted large crowds of poorer people, which some people saw as a threat to public order and a source of theft. People who owned property close to theatres often opposed them for this reason.

The government's attitude to the theatre

- The government worried that the content of plays might encourage rebellion.
- Under Queen Elizabeth, political and religious subjects were forbidden on stage.
- From 1572 published plays required a licence, which prevented them from addressing political issues.
- In 1574 the Common Council of the City of London issued a statement describing how the theatre brought 'corruptions of youth and other enormities' and 'great disorder'.
- By 1596 all theatres were banned from presenting plays in the City of London. All theatres had to move south of the River Thames.

Now try this

Give **two** reasons why people were concerned about the theatre in Elizabethan times.

Reasons for the increase in poverty

There were many reasons why poverty and vagabondage increased in Elizabethan England, including population growth, bad harvests, sheep farming and enclosure.

What was poverty during Elizabeth's reign?

- ✓ Spending more than 80 per cent of your income on bread
- ✓ Being unemployed or ill, so you could no longer provide for yourself or your family
- ✓ Being unable to afford the rising cost of food
- ✓ Needing financial help (poor relief) or charity (alms)

Vagrants were people without a settled home or regular work. Many vagrants were also seen as vagabonds – idle and dishonest people who wandered from place to place, committing crimes.

What types of people were poor?

Studies of parish records suggest that the poor fell into the following groupings.

- **Widows** or **women abandoned by their husbands and their families**, as women were paid very little.
- **The sick and the elderly** who were unable to work.
- **Orphaned children** – 40 per cent of the poor were under 16 years old.
- **People on low wages.**
- **Itinerants, vagrants and vagabonds** – homeless people who moved from their parishes looking for work. They were often involved in crimes and worried those in authority in Elizabethan England.

Population growth. The population of England grew from 3 million in 1551, to 4.2 million by 1601. This increased demand for food (driving up prices) while increasing the labour supply (driving down wages). This meant many ordinary people could no longer provide for themselves or their families.

Growth of towns between 1500 and 1600, such as London and Norwich, drove up the cost of rents, while food prices rose as food had to be brought in from rural areas to be sold.

Bad harvests (in 1562, 1565, 1573, 1586 and the 1590s) hit subsistence farmers (those who ate what they grew), reduced the food supply and drove up prices.

Reasons for the increase in poverty in Elizabethan England

Increasing demand for land. As the population increased more people needed land. This drove up rents and resulted in entry fees (up-front sums paid at the start of land rental). Many people could not afford to pay these.

Sheep farming. The growth of the wool trade after 1500 meant that many farmers preferred to rear sheep rather than grow food.

Enclosure. From 1500 onwards land was divided into fields for animal husbandry, arable farming or both ('up and down farming'), and given to farmers who farmed for profit. This denied people use of common land (land that could be used by everyone), which meant they were unable to provide for their families.

Economic recessions in the 1580s caused by trade restrictions, such as those involving Spain over the Netherlands, created unemployment and poverty.

Monasteries had provided help for the poor until their dissolution under Henry VIII in the 1530s. Now those struggling had no support.

Enclosure drove many people off the land altogether, leaving them with nowhere to live or farm. They became itinerants and vagrants.

Now try this

You need to consider other causes of poverty as well as population growth to answer this question.

How important was population growth in causing poverty in Elizabethan England? Write a paragraph to explain your ideas.

Attitudes to poverty

The Elizabethan government responded to the problem of poverty in different ways and, over time, attitudes towards the poor changed.

Traditional attitudes to poverty

Many Elizabethans distinguished between:

- the deserving or impotent poor (the old and the sick) who could not help themselves
- the idle poor (those who could work but chose not to do so).

It was felt the poor should be given every opportunity to better themselves. Those who refused to do so should be punished.

Many Elizabethans remained suspicious of the poor and demonised them as counterfeits and criminals. Vagrants and vagabonds who deceived or threatened the public were dealt with severely: they could be whipped, imprisoned, enslaved or even hanged if caught begging.

Reasons why attitudes to the poor were changing

Attitudes towards the poor changed during Elizabethan times. There were various reasons for this:

- the fear that poverty led to disorder and was a potential cause of rebellion
- the cost of dealing with the poor, especially the poor rates
- population changes and enclosure meant the poor were an increasingly visible presence in Elizabethan England
- changing economic circumstances, including problems with the wool trade, bad harvests and enclosure, forced the authorities (Crown, Parliament and Justices of the Peace) to develop a more constructive attitude towards poverty.

Policies towards the poor in Elizabethan times

Action	Type of change	Detail
Poor rate	**Continuity** – these measures existed before Elizabeth's reign and continued throughout Tudor times.	A local tax organised by Justices of the Peace (JPs), with the proceeds spent on improving the lives of the poor. The poor were given money or things to make and sell.
Charity		Often funded by local wealthy people, who gave their name to the charitable foundation – e.g. Lady Cecil's Bequest for Poor Tradesmen, Romford.
Statute of Artificers, 1563	**Progressive** – government's response to increased unemployment caused by falls in the wool trade.	Those refusing to pay the poor rates could be put in prison. Officials who failed to organise poor relief could pay a penalty of up to £20.
1576 Poor Relief Act		JPs were required to provide the poor with wool and raw materials, to enable them to make and sell things. The poor who refused to do so were sent to a special prison known as the house of correction.
1572 Vagabonds Act	**Repressive** change that targeted vagrants. Parliament felt vagrants posed a threat to public order and had to be deterred through harsh punishment. Yet the Act also recognised the need to help the poor by providing them with work.	Vagrants were: • whipped and had a hole drilled through each ear as a mark of shame, to warn others of their vagrancy • imprisoned if arrested again for vagrancy • given the death penalty for a third offence. The Act introduced a national poor rate, to provide support, including money and work, for the impotent poor. JPs had to keep a register of the poor. Those in authority (JPs, parish councils, and so on) were tasked with finding work for the able-bodied poor.
1601 Elizabethan Poor Law	**Administrative** change that standardised the treatment of the poor across England.	• Impotent poor cared for in almshouses/poorhouses • Able-bodied poor to work in a 'house of industry' (workhouse) • Idle poor sent to a 'house of correction'/prison • Pauper (poor) children became apprentices.

Now try this

Explain, using examples, how attitudes to the poor changed during Elizabeth's reign.

Government action

Poverty was a major problem during Elizabeth I's reign, as it placed a growing financial burden on communities and carried the risk of rebellion. The Elizabethan government was concerned about the increasing numbers of the poor and acted to resolve the issue for a range of different reasons.

As the number of poor people increased, **it became increasingly expensive to look after the poor**, especially in the 1590s after poor harvests. This put a financial burden on taxpayers who, under the terms of the 1572 Poor Law, had to pay the Poor Law Tax to provide relief for the poor. The government therefore needed to act to reduce this tax burden.

You can revise the government's policies towards the poor on page 13.

Many Elizabethans felt threatened by the poor, whom they saw as a potential threat to their property and safety as well as a source of rebellion. This was particularly the case in the 1590s when poor harvests and falling wages led to unrest in the countryside, especially in Oxfordshire and Devon. Government action was needed to control the poor and prevent future rebellions.

> **Why did the government take action in response to the increase in poverty?**

Attitudes towards the poor had changed. Before the Reformation in the 1530s (when the English Church became Protestant), people had felt a responsibility to provide alms (charity) for the poor as a way of shortening their time in Purgatory (a place Catholics believe you go to after death). However, the dissolution of the monasteries under Henry VIII had led to a decline in these Christian values and so people were less sympathetic towards the poor in the Elizabethan period.

The poor became increasingly visible in many Elizabethan towns, provoking hostility from wealthier people. This hostility was reinforced by stereotypes of the poor and vagrants that suggested they were both threatening and deceitful. This meant that many beggars were physically attacked and driven out of town, again putting pressure on the government to act.

The seriousness of the problem

> Poverty was a growing problem in Elizabethan England.

⬇

> The population of England increased from 3 000 000 in 1551 to 4 200 000 by 1601.

⬇

> This situation was made worse by rising prices and a debased coinage (the falling value of money).

⬇

> Many people, even in work, could no longer afford to provide for themselves and their families.

Poverty was particularly bad in London, which during Elizabeth's reign became the most heavily populated city in Europe. London was a magnet for the poor, who flocked there from elsewhere looking for work. This created a serious problem with vagrancy.

The effectiveness of government action

The Elizabethan government put various measures in place to deal with the poor and these had some success in reducing poverty.

👍 Poor relief became the responsibility of government, including local governments, especially parishes, rather than individual charities. This meant the poor were provided for and did not starve. As a result, even in the 1590s when harvests were poor, there was no rebellion or disorder.

👍 Elizabethan poor laws, especially the Poor Law Act of 1601, remained in place for a long time, suggesting that the legislation was successful.

👎 However, government measures failed to tackle the underlying causes of poverty: low wages; enclosure; poor harvests; a rising population. This meant the problem of poverty continued throughout the 17th and 18th centuries.

You can refer to this page and page 13 when answering this question.

Now try this

Explain why government attempts to reduce poverty during the Elizabethan period were successful. Give **two** reasons.

Hawkins and Drake

John Hawkins and Francis Drake were English sailors involved in exploration, the looting of Spanish ships, the sale of goods in West Africa and the slave trade – selling African slaves in the West Indies.

John Hawkins, 1532–1595

- Hawkins was England's first slave trader.
- In 1562 he sailed from Plymouth with three ships and violently kidnapped about 400 West Africans, later selling them on as slaves in the West Indies.
- Between 1562 and 1567 Hawkins and his cousin Francis Drake made three voyages to West Africa and enslaved between 1200 and 1400 Africans. They kidnapped villagers, sometimes with the help of native Africans.
- Hawkins then crossed the Atlantic and sold his 'cargo' to the Spanish.

Many Africans died on the voyage owing to the terrible conditions in which they were kept.

The slave trade involving West Africa and the West Indies was known as the **triangular trade**. Those involved in the trade made huge profits from selling the people they kidnapped into a life of slavery as well as from the sugar and tobacco produced on slave plantations.

Hawkins was unashamed of his part in the slave trade. His coat of arms showed a bound slave.

Francis Drake (c1540–1596)

- Drake was an English sea captain, privateer, navigator, slave trader and politician.
- He carried out the second circumnavigation of the world, from 1577 to 1580.
- He began an era of privateering and piracy on the western coast of the Americas – an area that previously had been free of piracy.

Engraving of Drake, c1583. The globe refers to his circumnavigation of the world.

Colonisation means of settling in and taking control of a foreign country.

Why were voyages of exploration made during Elizabethan times?

Expanding territory. Voyages of exploration enabled explorers to claim territory for Elizabeth's government, especially in the New World, leading to settlement and **colonisation**.

Private investment. Private investors, including Elizabeth I ('the Crown') and her courtiers, funded many of the voyages of discovery. Although this was risky, the rewards could be enormous.

Improvements in ship design. Ships or galleons had bigger sails, were faster and easier to move, and had greater firepower against attack by pirates. They also were more stable and could take on more supplies, encouraging longer voyages and exploration.

Trade. English merchants needed new trading opportunities, as war with Spain and in the Netherlands had severely damaged the wool and cloth trades.

The development of standardised maps such as the Mercator Map of 1569 meant sailors and traders could be confident they were going in the right direction. This reduced the risks of exploration and encouraged further voyages.

New technology. The development of devices such as quadrants and astrolabes made navigation more precise, so voyages were safer and faster, leading to more exploration and trade.

Adventure. Some young Elizabethan men such as Francis Drake set off on voyages of discovery and exploration. Their published accounts of these voyages, though often inaccurate, persuaded others to venture into the unknown in the belief that fortunes could be made.

Now try this

Give **two** reasons why Drake and Hawkins were important figures in the development of exploration and trade in Elizabethan times.

Circumnavigation, 1577–1580

Between December 1577 and September 1580, Francis Drake **circumnavigated** (sailed around) the globe. After his voyage, he was knighted by Queen Elizabeth and became Sir Francis Drake.

The Portuguese explorer Ferdinand Magellan carried out the first circumnavigation of the globe, between 1519 and 1522.

Why did Drake circumnavigate the globe?

☑ **He was attacking Spain.** Drake did not aim to sail around the world. His main purpose was to raid Spanish colonies in the Pacific, as relations with Spain were declining at this time.

☑ **Revenge.** The Spanish had attacked Drake's fleet at St Juan de Ulúa and most of his men had been killed.

☑ **Profit.** Loot, booty and trade meant there were huge profits to be made from Drake's proposed journey to the Americas and beyond, so people were willing to invest in the expedition, including Elizabeth I.

Drake's circumnavigation

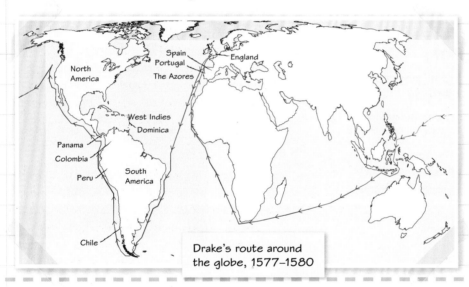

Drake's route around the globe, 1577–1580

For more on Sir Francis Drake and why voyages of exploration were made during the Elizabethan period, turn to page 15. To revise Drake's turbulent relationship with Spain, see page 29.

England's reputation as a seafaring power increased – in spite of the fact that only one of Drake's five ships, *Golden Hind*, survived the voyage. Drake had overcome considerable difficulties in sailing around the globe.

Drake's expedition resulted in Nova Albion, an area near San Francisco, being claimed as English territory, with Elizabeth as its queen. This encouraged further trade and exploration, especially to the New World, where colonies were established in New England in the late 16th and early 17th centuries.

England's naval power increased as a way of defending the country from invasion and protecting its trading interests.

The benefits of Drake's circumnavigation of the globe

Drake's achievement boosted the income of Elizabeth and her government. This improved England's status as a European power. It also made her a potential ally for other European states who saw Spain as a rival power.

English ships began to trade elsewhere – in China, West Africa and India. This established England as a major trading power.

Now try this

Give **three** reasons why England benefitted from Drake's circumnavigation of the world.

Voyages and trade

One of the key purposes of Elizabethan exploration was to open up profitable trading routes, including the Northwest Passage and routes to West Africa, the Americas and the Far East.

The search for the Northwest Passage

Martin Frobisher made three voyages in search of a north-western route to China and the Far East:

- The first left in 1576 and reached Greenland.
- The second, in 1577, again reached Baffin Island, (now in Canada), but found nothing of value.
- A third expedition, in 1578, was completely unsuccessful and Frobisher returned to England with little of value.

Three further expeditions by John Davis (1585–1587) were equally unsuccessful.

Attempts to colonise the Americas

Expeditions to colonise the east coast of America were unsuccessful:

- An expedition in 1578 by Humphrey Gilbert was abandoned. His second, in 1583, reached Newfoundland, but many of the colonists fell ill and Gilbert himself died on the way home.
- Attempts to settle colonists in Virginia, on Roanoke Island (from 1585) also came to nothing. The colony was mysteriously abandoned.

West Africa and the triangular trade

The slave trader John Hawkins helped establish the triangular trade. This involved:

- selling goods in West Africa
- purchasing slaves in West Africa and selling them in the West Indies
- buying sugar, tobacco and cotton in the West Indies and returning to England.

This trade was strengthened when the Barbary Company, which traded off the West Coast of Africa, was established in 1585.

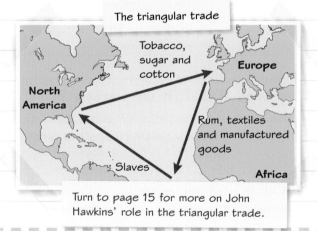

The triangular trade

Tobacco, sugar and cotton

Europe

North America

Rum, textiles and manufactured goods

Slaves

Africa

Turn to page 15 for more on John Hawkins' role in the triangular trade.

Trade in the Far East

- In 1582, Elizabeth I sent Ralph Fitch to be ambassador to the Emperor of China. He was captured by the Portuguese but managed to escape, travelling through northern India, Burma and Malaya before returning to England in 1591. His account of his travels showed that profitable trade in the East was possible.
- The **Levant Company** was set up in 1592 to trade with the Eastern Mediterranean. It supplied the English market with Turkish carpets, Mediterranean fruits and Persian silks, as well as spices and luxury goods. It successfully exported textiles to the Turks.
- In 1600 the **East India Company** was set up to trade with China, India and the East in cotton, silk, salt, tea and opium. It encouraged merchants and aristocrats to invest in these trading opportunities. By the late 17th century it dominated trade between England and India and had its own private army and trading ships.

The Crown benefitted by charging duties (taxes) on imported goods. It also made money by granting trading licences to organisations like the Barbary Company and the East India Company.

English traders and merchants made big profits from trading with other countries.

How did England benefit from exploration and trade?

Trade allowed new goods, including potatoes, tobacco, coffee, spices and dried grapes, to enter English markets.

Now try this

Describe **two** ways in which exploration and trade were important to the Elizabethan economy.

Sir Walter Raleigh

Walter Raleigh was an influential courtier and explorer throughout Elizabeth I's reign.

Walter Raleigh (c1552–1618)

- He took part in a military expedition to Ireland in 1580. This gained him enormous favour with Elizabeth I and he was given land there following the defeat of a local rebellion.

- In 1584, Queen Elizabeth granted Raleigh a royal charter for seven years, which allowed him to explore, take over and rule any lands that were not Christian or ruled by Christians in return for one-fifth of all the gold and silver mined there. In 1587 he was named Captain of the Queen's Guard, the highest office at court.

- The royal charter enabled Raleigh to organise and make money from expeditions to the New World.

Walter Raleigh was an English nobleman and explorer, and a favourite of Queen Elizabeth.

Expeditions to the New World

1585: after a first fact-finding expedition in 1584, 107 settlers set out for Roanoke, Virginia, in North America.

1586: colonists return to England, abandoning Virginia.

1587: a new group of settlers sets sail for Roanoke.

1590: English sailors find Roanoke abandoned. What happened remains a mystery.

No further colonisation takes place until the early 17th century.

Other expeditions

1595: leads an expedition to the Orinoco river basin in South America, in search of the 'city of gold', El Dorado.

1595: attacks the Spanish coast, capturing the merchant ship *Mother of God*.

1596–1597: takes part in the capture of Cadiz, as well as raids on Spanish bases in the Azores.

1616: leads a second expedition to South America in search of El Dorado.

Raleigh is executed in 1618 for attacking Spanish shipping against the king's wishes.

Raleigh and Elizabeth

Raleigh's relationship with Elizabeth changed between 1580 and 1603.

- Military success in Ireland in 1580 made him a favourite, and Elizabeth granted him lands and made him a Captain of the Guard.

- He fell out of favour in 1592 for secretly marrying one of the queen's maids of honour, Elizabeth Throckmorton, and was expelled from court and sent to the Tower.

- Later military expeditions to Spain, leading to the capture of Cadiz in 1597, and South America, were an attempt to win back the queen's favour. This seemed to work as he was made Governor of Jersey in 1600.

Why was Raleigh important?

☑ He encouraged exploration and colonisation of the New World by getting investors (aristocrats and merchants) to fund expeditions. This set an example and led to further expeditions.

☑ Raleigh's failures, especially at Roanoke, Virginia, changed the way English governments approached colonisation. While Raleigh raised money among his friends, future colonisation used Joint Stock Companies, where investors bought shares in expeditions. These companies paid a share of the profits to the shareholders. This led to more investment.

Now try this

In no more than **two** paragraphs, explain how Raleigh's actions contributed to the settlement of the New World.

The question of religion

Elizabeth's religious settlement meant that England became a Protestant country again and Catholics were seen increasingly as a threat.

The differences between Catholicism, Protestantism and Puritanism

	Catholics ('old religion')	Protestants ('new religion')	Puritans (strict Protestants)
Beliefs	Pope is head of the Church helped by cardinals, bishops and priests	No pope; it may be necessary to have archbishops or bishops	No popes, cardinals or bishops
	Church is intermediary (go-between) between God and people; can forgive sins	Personal direct relationship with God via prayer and Bible; only God can forgive sins	
	During Mass bread and wine become actual body and blood of Christ (transubstantiation)	Bread and wine simply represent the body and blood of Christ; there is no miracle.	
	7 sacraments (ceremonies)	2 sacraments: Baptism and Holy Communion	
	Priests are celibate	Priests can marry	
Practices	Services in Latin	Services in English	
	Priests wear vestments	Priests wear simple vestments	
	Churches highly decorated	Churches plain and simple	Churches whitewashed with no decorations
Support	Catholics the majority in north and west England	Mostly south-east England (London, Kent, East Anglia)	Puritans found in London and East Anglia

Religious divisions in England before the Elizabethan settlement

- The Reformation divided the Christian Church between Catholics and Protestants from 1532 onwards. Catholics remained true to the Catholic Church in Rome, led by the pope, while Protestants no longer recognised the pope's authority.

- Henry VIII declared that he was Head of the Church in England and dissolved the monasteries; however, many of Henry's religious beliefs were Catholic. Edward VI moved England further towards Protestantism while Mary Tudor made England Catholic again.

- From the 1530s, many Protestants came to England to escape persecution in Europe. They settled in London, East Anglia and Kent.

- The north of England remained largely Catholic. There was a risk that Catholics in the north could rebel in order to overthrow Elizabeth and restore Catholicism.

- Some English Protestants became Puritans – strict Protestants with extreme views who wanted to purify the Christian religion by getting rid of anything that was not in the Bible. They first appeared in the 1560s and increased in number during Elizabeth's reign.

The Act of Uniformity established the appearance of churches and how religious services were to be held. It required everyone to attend church.

The Act of Supremacy: Elizabeth became Supreme Governor (Head) of the Church of England. All clergy and royal officials had to swear an oath of allegiance to her.

Key features of Elizabeth's religious settlement of 1559

The Royal Injunctions: This was a set of instructions to the clergy which included rules about how to worship God and how to conduct services.

An **Ecclesiastical** (Church) High Commission was established to keep discipline within the Church and enforce Elizabeth's religious settlement. Disloyal clergy could be punished.

The Book of Common Prayer (1559) introduced a set church service to be used in all churches. The clergy had to follow the Prayer Book wording during services or be punished.

Now try this

Give **two** reasons why Catholics would have opposed Elizabeth's religious settlement of 1559.

The Northern Rebellion

The Northern Rebellion (1569–1570, sometimes called the Revolt of the Northern Earls) was a key turning point in Elizabeth's reign.

Why did the Northern Earls rebel?

- The earls and their followers wanted to make England Catholic again. They especially resented the appointment of James Pilkington, a Protestant, as Bishop of Durham in 1561.
- The earls had lost much of their influence at court under Elizabeth. They resented the 'new men', such as William Cecil, John Forster and Robert Dudley.
- Elizabeth's refusal to name an heir, or to marry and have a child, created uncertainty. The earls feared civil war and loss of power and wealth under a future Protestant monarch.

The key players in the Northern Rebellion

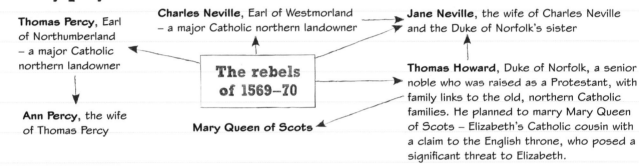

Thomas Percy, Earl of Northumberland – a major Catholic northern landowner

Ann Percy, the wife of Thomas Percy

Charles Neville, Earl of Westmorland – a major Catholic northern landowner

The rebels of 1569–70

Mary Queen of Scots

Jane Neville, the wife of Charles Neville and the Duke of Norfolk's sister

Thomas Howard, Duke of Norfolk, a senior noble who was raised as a Protestant, with family links to the old, northern Catholic families. He planned to marry Mary Queen of Scots – Elizabeth's Catholic cousin with a claim to the English throne, who posed a significant threat to Elizabeth.

The marriage plan

- Mary would marry the Duke of Norfolk, depose (remove) Elizabeth and become queen herself. She told the Spanish Ambassador in 1569 that she 'shall be Queen of England in three months' and that 'Mass shall be said all over the country'.
- Robert Dudley told Elizabeth of the plan, leading to Norfolk's arrest and imprisonment in the Tower.

Progress of the revolt

- Northumberland and Westmorland, with their wives' support, continued with the revolt. They took control of Durham Cathedral, celebrating Mass there, as well as in other northern churches, and began to move south.
- Elizabeth moved Mary to Coventry, to stop her escaping to join the rebels.
- Though the rebels captured Hartlepool, support from Spain never arrived.

Why did the revolt fail?

- Support from Spain never arrived.
- Many northern landowners, especially those in Lancashire and Cheshire, remained loyal to Elizabeth.
- Many landowners did not want to risk losing wealth gained from the dissolution of the monasteries under Henry VIII by backing a failed revolt.

The revolt's significance

- Mary was not directly involved but the revolt showed that she could not be trusted – and she remained in prison.
- The pope excommunicated Elizabeth and called on Catholics to depose her, encouraging more plots.
- England's Catholics could not be trusted so the government took harsh steps against them.
- Elizabeth's control over the north of England was strengthened.

Those involved in the plot suffered different fates. Thomas Percy was executed, while Charles Neville fled abroad. The Duke of Norfolk was imprisoned and later pardoned.

Now try this

In no more than two paragraphs, explain why the Northern Rebellion threatened Elizabeth's position as monarch in 1569.

Elizabeth's excommunication

Elizabeth's excommunication in 1570 was a turning point because it established that Catholics were a threat both to Elizabeth and her religious settlement.

Why were Catholics seen as a threat?

- **Catholics owed their allegiance to the pope** rather than the queen, and were therefore seen as disloyal to Elizabeth.

- **Religious wars in Europe** and the massacre of Protestants, especially in France and the Spanish Netherlands, caused many Protestants to worry they would be treated similarly if Catholicism were restored in England. People had not forgotten Mary I's brutal treatment of Protestants (many were burned alive).

- **Catholics were active in plots and rebellions** against Elizabeth, both in England (the Northern Rebellion) and Ireland (Desmond Rebellions of 1569–1573 and 1579–1583).

John Rogers, a Protestant, being burned alive at the stake during Mary I's reign. This image, from *Foxe's Book of Martyrs* (published 1563), convinced many Protestants, especially Puritans, that Catholics were a threat.

The Catholic threat was greatest in the 1570s and 1580s when there were a number of plots and conspiracies against Elizabeth.

The papal bull of excommunication, 1570

- *Regnans in Excelsis* (meaning 'reigning on high') was a papal bull issued by Pope Pius V on 25 February 1570.

- It declared Elizabeth a **heretic** (someone who openly disagrees with approved Church teachings), calling her 'the pretended Queen of England and the servant of crime'.

- It released all Elizabeth's subjects from allegiance (loyalty) to her – they no longer had to obey their queen.

- Pope Gregory VIII suspended the bull in 1580 but Pope Sixtus V renewed it in 1588.

Pope Pius V issued the papal bull that excommunicated Elizabeth I.

The consequences of the papal bull

It encouraged Catholic states, such as France and Spain, to believe they could make war on England and support plots to overthrow Elizabeth as monarch.

The papal bull was a turning point because:

English treatment of Catholics became more severe.

It encouraged further plots against Elizabeth centred on Mary Queen of Scots.

A **recusant** was a Catholic who refused to attend Church of England services on the grounds they were heretical (against the true teachings of the Catholic Church).

Why things got worse for Catholics

After 1570, Elizabeth's government began to pass laws reducing the rights of Catholics:

- The Mass (a Catholic service) was banned.

- Devotional items such as rosary beads were treated with suspicion.

- **Recusants** were fined heavily.

- Catholic priests were arrested and were often tortured before being executed.

Catholics were now seen as the 'enemy within' and were closely monitored. For example, Francis Walsingham intercepted their correspondence to uncover plots against Elizabeth.

Now try this

In **one** paragraph, explain why Catholics were treated more harshly after the papal bull of 1570.

Catholic plots 1

The Catholic threat to Elizabeth intensified after 1570. The Ridolfi plot of 1571 was one of a number of Catholic plots against her. Then, in 1580, a Catholic mission led by Edmund Campion arrived in England and started preaching against the English Protestant Church.

The progress of the Ridolfi plot

1 Roberto Ridolfi was an Italian banker who lived in England and worked as a spy for the pope.

2 In 1571, Ridolfi plotted to murder Elizabeth, start a Spanish invasion and put Mary Queen of Scots on the English throne. Mary would then marry the Duke of Norfolk.

3 In March 1571, Ridolfi discussed the plot with the pope, Philip II of Spain and the Duke of Alba, in the Netherlands (controlled by Spain). Ridolfi had a letter signed by the Duke of Norfolk in which Norfolk declared himself a Catholic and pledged to lead the rebellion with Philip II's support.

4 Philip II instructed the Duke of Alba to prepare 10000 troops to send across the English Channel in support of the revolt.

5 Sir William Cecil discovered the plot and, by autumn 1571, was able to prove that Norfolk was guilty of high treason (plotting against Elizabeth). Ridolfi never returned to England.

6 When Parliament met in May 1572, it demanded the execution of both Norfolk and Mary Queen of Scots. Elizabeth signed Norfolk's death warrant, leading to his execution in June 1572. However, Elizabeth was reluctant to punish Mary, and refused to remove her from the succession. Executing Mary would further anger English Catholics and might unite France and Spain (Europe's two big Catholic monarchies) against her.

It confirmed that English Catholics and Mary Queen of Scots remained a threat to Elizabeth.

It reinforced the threat from Spain, as Philip II would support any plots against Elizabeth.

The significance of the Ridolfi plot

The threat from Spain meant that England needed to improve relations with France, as England could not fight both countries at once.

The government now began to monitor Catholics more closely and treat them more severely. Two laws passed in 1581 meant that families could be fined for sheltering priests and charged with treason if they converted people to Catholicism.

Jesuits were a Catholic group from Spain that tried to make everyone Catholic.

Campion's mission

- In 1580, Jesuit missionaries led by Edmund Campion and Robert Persons arrived in England from Europe, aiming to restore Catholicism.

- Campion and Persons were English Catholics who had spent time abroad. They began to preach and to distribute leaflets. They claimed their motives were purely religious.

- The mission was very secretive. Catholic priests had to hide in **priest's holes** (hidden spaces in houses) so they would not be discovered.

- However, Campion insisted on **recusancy** – Catholics must not attend Protestant services. This challenged Elizabeth's position as Head of the Church in England.

- Their punishment was severe: 130 priests including Campion were charged with treason. Campion was hung, drawn and quartered in December 1581. 64 Catholic priests were executed between 1581 and 1588. Some priests were persuaded to become government informers, leading to further arrests of Catholics by the authorities.

- This treatment shows that English Catholics, particularly Jesuits, were now seen as the greatest threat to Elizabeth.

Now try this

Write a paragraph to explain why Catholics, and Jesuits in particular, were treated severely in Elizabethan England after 1570.

Catholic plots 2

The Throckmorton and Babington plots were organised by Catholics against Elizabeth.

The Throckmorton plot, 1583

The plot	Significance
• The French Duke of Guise, a cousin of Mary Queen of Scots, plotted to invade England and overthrow Elizabeth, free Mary and make England Catholic again. • Philip II offered to help pay for the revolt and the Pope approved of the plan. • Francis Throckmorton, a young Englishman, would pass letters between the plotters and Mary. • Sir Francis Walsingham, Elizabeth's Secretary of State, discovered the plot in May 1583. • In November 1583, Walsingham's spies found papers at Throckmorton's house revealing his part in the conspiracy. He was arrested and tortured. He confessed and was executed in May 1584.	• It revealed the extent of the Catholic threat from foreign Catholic powers such as France and Spain, English Catholics and Mary Queen of Scots. • Throckmorton's papers included a list of Catholic sympathisers in England. The government now treated English Catholics with greater suspicion. Many left England. Others were imprisoned, watched or kept under house arrest. An Act of Parliament of 1581 made helping Catholic priests punishable by death.

The Babington plot, 1586

The plot	Significance

• The Duke of Guise planned to invade England, murder Elizabeth and put Mary Queen of Scots on the throne. Again, Philip II and the pope supported the plot.
• Anthony Babington, a Catholic, wrote to Mary in July 1586 about the conspiracy.
• Sir Francis Walsingham intercepted and read Babington's letters to Mary, which clearly demonstrated her involvement in the plot.
• Babington and the plotters were sentenced to death and were hung, drawn and quartered.
• In October 1586, Mary was sentenced to death for her part in the plot. Elizabeth delayed, but signed Mary's death warrant in February 1587. Mary was beheaded shortly afterwards.
	• Elizabeth's situation was insecure – more so than with previous plots. This was because:
	  ○ by 1585, England and Spain were close to war
	  ○ the Treaty of Joinville meant England could no longer rely on France as an ally
	  ○ both French and Spanish Catholics were involved in the plot, increasing the threat.
	• Elizabeth's government became determined to crush the Catholic threat and the persecution of Catholics intensified:
	  ○ In 1585, 11 000 Catholics were imprisoned or placed under house arrest.
	  ○ In 1586, 31 priests were executed.
	  ○ The execution of Mary Queen of Scots ended all hopes of replacing Elizabeth with a Catholic queen.

Elizabeth's government used agents provocateurs to encourage Babington and his conspirators to provide details of the plot.

Government suspicion of Catholics deepened. This was because no Catholic could be loyal to Elizabeth when their religion demanded they should be loyal to the pope first.

Catholic conspiracies were dealt with severely. The threat posed by Catholics to Elizabeth and her religious settlement of 1559 was serious. Catholics were plotting with foreign powers to overthrow the queen and return England to Catholicism.

The consequences of Catholic plots and conspiracies

Laws passed against Catholics became stricter. For example, an Act of 1585 made sheltering a Catholic priest punishable by death.

Catholics became very secretive. By the 1580s Catholics sheltered priests in priest's holes and conducted worship in secret.

Now try this

Describe **two** ways in which life as a Catholic in Elizabethan England became harder as a result of the Catholic plots.

Puritans and Puritanism

Many radical Protestants, or Puritans, challenged Elizabeth's religious settlement of 1559, but the Puritan threat had declined by the end of Elizabeth's reign.

Who were the Puritans?

Puritans were radical Protestants who wanted to 'purify' the Christian religion by getting rid of anything that wasn't in the Bible.

- Puritans wanted to develop their own Church, which would not be controlled by the queen. There would be no bishops, and priests would not wear **vestments**.

- Puritans wanted to make the world a 'more godly' place by banning 'sinful' activities, such as attending the theatre, gambling and cock fighting.

- Puritans saw hard work and making money as a sign of God's favour. They expected the poor to work hard to get themselves out of poverty and not rely on charity.

- Puritans wanted a simpler style of worship, whitewashed churches and no 'graven images' (worship of religious idols), including crucifixes and statues, which were seen as ungodly and too Catholic.

- A minority of Puritans believed the monarch could be overthrown in certain circumstances. This was especially the case if the monarch was Catholic.

Vestments were special clothing worn by clergy during worship.

A Puritan family – the father is teaching his wife and children.

- Many Puritans were anti-Catholic and believed the pope was the 'anti-Christ'. Other Puritans – **millenarians** – believed the world was ending and that Christians had to prepare for Jesus' return.

Puritan views varied. Some Puritans were relatively moderate and just wanted a simpler style of worship. Others, such as John Stubbs and Thomas Cartwright, wanted more far-reaching changes that challenged the authority of Elizabeth's government.

There were growing numbers of **Puritans in England** and a significant number of MPs were Puritan. This Puritan Choir (a group of Puritans in the House of Commons) could challenge the government's authority and the monarch's control of the Church.

Why were the Puritans a threat to Elizabeth's government?

Some bishops and archbishops including Edmund Grindal (Archbishop of Canterbury from 1575 to 1583) were sympathetic to Puritan ideas.

Puritan tracts (pamphlets distributed to the public) could be critical of the queen and the Church of England. For example, the **Martin Marprelate tracts** accused the queen and her government of being 'anti-Christian'. Such comments challenged the authority of the Church of England and Elizabeth as Head of the Church, so might encourage rebellion. As Archbishop Parker stated, Puritan ideas would 'undo the queen and all others that depended upon her'.

Some Puritans challenged Elizabeth's religious settlement of 1559. They tried to make changes to Church practices without the queen's permission, so weakening her authority. For example, the Lambeth Articles of 1595 set out Church thinking (or theology) and included Puritan beliefs, but senior clergy passed them without the queen's approval. When she found out, Elizabeth was furious and demanded they be withdrawn immediately.

The Puritan threat decreased towards the end of Elizabeth's reign, as John Whitgift, then Archbishop of Canterbury, took steps to reduce the Puritan influence within the Church.

Now try this

Give **two** reasons why the Puritans were a threat to Elizabeth's government.

Response to religious matters

Attitudes towards Puritanism varied but by the late 1580s it was being discouraged.

Attitudes and actions of Elizabeth and her government

Elizabeth remained suspicious of Puritan thinking and practices. She disliked:

- the idea of predestination
- Puritan practices, especially their reluctance to wear vestments, as this challenged the religious settlement of 1559
- Puritan preaching or 'prophesying', which she thought encouraged disobedience within the Church.

The Puritan response

Many Puritans, including John Penry and Job Throckmorton, ignored Elizabeth's wishes and produced religious tracts condemning her government. Others, including John Field, Walter Travers and Thomas Cartwright, tried to work within the Church to ensure that Puritan ideas were adopted.

The attitude of Archbishop Parker

- Matthew Parker was Archbishop of Canterbury between 1559 and 1575.
- He tried to ensure the Church of England conformed to the 1559 religious settlement.
- Parker's Book of Advertisements (1566) required clergy, including Puritans, to wear vestments, as stated in the 1559 settlement.

See page 24 for more on Puritan tracts that were critical of the Elizabethan government.

Archbishop Grindal

Edmund Grindal was Archbishop of Canterbury between 1575 and 1583. He was reluctant to persecute Puritans.

In 1577, Elizabeth stated that she wanted to discourage Puritan clergy preaching and holding meetings. Grindal was reluctant to do this.

In 1577, Grindal had his authority as archbishop suspended. It was only fully reinstated in 1582.

Many Puritans admired Archbishop Grindal (left) for his willingness to stand up to Queen Elizabeth, while Archbishop Whitgift (right) opposed Puritans and introduced measures to end their religious practices.

The policies of Archbishop Whitgift

John Whitgift was Archbishop of Canterbury between 1583 and 1604, and a Privy Councillor. He opposed Puritans, especially those who spoke out against Elizabeth and her religious settlement of 1559.

1 He increased the powers of the Church Court of High Commission so the Court could take action against Puritan clergy. In 1589 the Court banned Puritan preaching in London parishes and Puritan printing presses were closed down.

2 He persuaded Parliament to pass the Act against Seditious Sectaries (1593), which made Puritanism an offence. Puritans could no longer distribute leaflets promoting their ideas.

3 Action was taken to silence Puritans. For example, Thomas Cartwright, a leading Puritan, was imprisoned because his ideas challenged the Act of Uniformity and the Religious Settlement of 1559. Another Puritan, Peter Wentworth, was imprisoned in the Tower in 1593 and died there.

4 As Privy Councillor he also helped ensure that Puritans who supported separation from the Church of England were dealt with harshly. For example, John Greenwood and Harry Barrowe were executed for this in 1593.

Whitgift's policies reduced the Puritan threat by the end of Elizabeth's reign.

Now try this

Explain **two** ways in which Archbishop Whitgift had reduced the Puritan threat by 1603.

Mary's arrival in England

Mary Queen of Scots had a legitimate claim to the English throne and was at the centre of many plots designed to overthrow Elizabeth.

Mary's claim to the throne

Mary Queen of Scots was Henry VII's great-granddaughter and Elizabeth's second cousin. She was descended from Margaret Tudor, Henry VIII's sister, was Catholic and had a legitimate claim to the English throne. Mary was married to the French king, Francis II, and inherited the Scottish crown when she was only six days old. While Mary was in France, her mother, Mary of Guise, ruled Scotland.

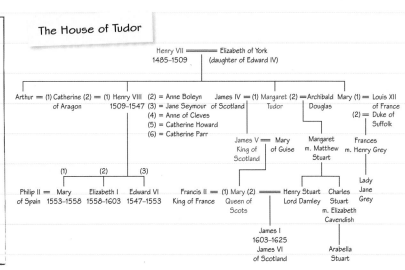

The House of Tudor

Why was Mary important?

- Mary was Catholic, which meant that many Catholics, including members of the nobility, would be prepared to support her as a monarch if Elizabeth was removed as queen.

- Mary's claim was strengthened by the fact there were no concerns about her legitimacy. Elizabeth's legitimacy was questioned by Catholics, however, as her mother Anne Boleyn's marriage to Henry VIII was seen by many Catholics as illegitimate. This undermined Elizabeth's claim to the throne.

- Mary would always be at the centre of, and often a willing participant in, Catholic plots and conspiracies against Elizabeth. These involved both English plotters and foreign powers.

Turn to pages 22–23 for more on plots against Elizabeth involving Mary Queen of Scots.

Mary leaves Scotland

On the death of Francis II in 1560, Mary had returned to Scotland and married Henry Stuart (Lord Darnley), producing an heir, James. Darnley was later murdered (possibly with Mary's involvement) and this time Mary married the Earl of Bothwell.

Many Scots assumed that Mary had murdered Darnley and, in 1568, they rebelled against her, imprisoned her and forced her to abdicate (give up her throne) in favour of her son, James. Mary escaped and raised an army, but this was defeated at Langside near Glasgow. Mary then fled to England, seeking her cousin Elizabeth's help against the Scottish rebels.

Mary's imprisonment in England, 1568

Mary was held in England in comfort but under guard while Elizabeth decided what to do with her. The Scottish rebels demanded that Mary be handed over and tried for the murder of Darnley.

Mary's arrival in England created a problem for Elizabeth. By remaining in England Mary could encourage rebellion, as many members of the Catholic nobility believed they could overthrow Elizabeth and place Mary on the throne. However, to take action against Mary, as an anointed monarch, would also reduce Elizabeth's own status, power and authority.

You could also use pages 20, 22 and 23 to help you answer this question.

Now try this

Explain **two** ways in which Mary Queen of Scot's arrival in England posed a problem for Elizabeth.

Mary's treatment in England

Relations between the two monarchs remained tense. Between 1568 and 1569 Elizabeth became increasingly concerned about the arrival of Mary Queen of Scots in England, and the threat she posed to her throne.

Elizabeth's options, from 1568 to 1569

Option	Possible problems
1 Help Mary to regain her throne	Helping Mary regain her throne would anger the Scottish nobility and leave Elizabeth facing a Catholic monarch on her northern border. The Auld Alliance with France could then be revived to threaten her.
2 Hand Mary over to the Scottish lords	Mary was the former wife of Francis II. Her trial, imprisonment and execution by Scottish noblemen with Elizabeth's permission could provoke France, driving them into alliance with Spain. This might lead both countries into war with England.
3 Allow Mary to go abroad	Allowing Mary to go abroad could see her return to France. This could provoke a French plot that aimed to remove Elizabeth from the English throne and replace her with Mary.
4 Keep Mary in England	Keeping Mary in England was probably the best option for Elizabeth. However, it carried the risk that Catholic plotters might try to overthrow Elizabeth and replace her with Mary.

The Casket Letters Affair

It was claimed that Mary had plotted with other members of the Scottish nobility, including her lover the Earl of Bothwell, to murder her husband Lord Darnley.

- A meeting was set up at York to hear the case against Mary between October 1568 and January 1569.

- The Scottish lords brought love letters with them, written by Mary to Bothwell. The letters apparently showed that Mary was guilty of murdering Lord Darnley, her second husband. The lords insisted that Mary should be handed over to face trial.

- Mary said that she could not be tried because she was an anointed monarch. She also refused to offer a plea unless Elizabeth guaranteed a verdict of innocence.

- Elizabeth refused, but she did not hand Mary over for trial.

By not handing over Mary, Elizabeth ensured:

👍 the Scottish nobility could not imprison or execute Mary

👍 the French would be satisfied

👍 her subjects did not punish an anointed monarch.

The conference did not reach any conclusions. Mary, therefore, stayed in England, in captivity. But she remained a threat, because any plots against Elizabeth, especially those involving Catholics, would seek to replace Elizabeth with Mary.

For more about the Catholic plots against Elizabeth, turn to pages 22 and 23.

Why did Elizabeth not make Mary her heir?

One further possibility was that Elizabeth would acknowledge Mary as her heir. However, to do so would upset English Protestants, including those on her Privy Council. Without the support of these Privy Councillors, Elizabeth – already distrusted by many Catholics – would have few supporters left. Moreover, the prospect of a Catholic heir would, in the event of Elizabeth's death, result in civil war.

For more about the role of the Privy Council, go to page 2.

Think about the options Elizabeth had and what their consequences might be.

Now try this

Why did Elizabeth keep Mary captive in England? Make **two** points and explain each one.

27

Removing Mary

Elizabeth I struggled to decide what to do with Mary Queen of Scots, but eventually signed her death warrant in February 1587. Mary was executed for a number of different reasons.

What to do with Mary?

Mary posed a complex and difficult challenge to Elizabeth's position as queen. However, there were limits to what Elizabeth could do.

If Mary remained in prison, she could continue to encourage rebellion. Mary was an alternative monarch in waiting, with a legitimate claim to the throne. She also had the support of many Catholics, especially in northern England.

If Elizabeth executed Mary, she would upset Spain and France, risking war and invasion. She would also be executing an anointed monarch, which would set a dangerous precedent (if it had been done once before, it could be done again). This would make Elizabeth and her heirs more vulnerable in future.

Having excommunicated Elizabeth, the pope would support any intervention by the Catholic kings of Europe to overthrow Elizabeth and put Mary on the throne.

Turn to page 26 for more on Mary's claim to the English throne and links to the French monarchy. For details of the Catholic plots involving Mary, see pages 22 and 23.

The attitude of Parliament by the 1580s

Many in Parliament were increasingly suspicious of Mary, owing to her Catholicism and involvement in plots against Elizabeth.

Elizabeth's government adopted a 'wait and see policy' towards Mary. They:
- continued to hold her prisoner
- sent out spies and agents provocateurs to discover her role in Catholic plots
- would take decisive action when there was enough evidence to charge her.

These fears increased after the Wars of Religion (1562–98) and the St Bartholomew's Day Massacre (1572) in France, where Catholics slaughtered many Protestants. Protestants in England feared a similar outcome if Mary became queen.

Mary had been involved in a series of plots against Elizabeth – the Northern Rebellion, the Ridolfi plot, the Throckmorton plot and the Babington plot.

In 1586, Walsingham's spies found evidence that Mary was involved with the Babington plotters. She was tried and convicted under the Act for Preservation of the Queen's Safety.

The Spanish threat of invasion was very real by 1587, and Philip II had been connected with previous plots involving Mary. This made keeping Mary alive too risky.

The pope supported any foreign invasion that would replace Elizabeth (whom he had excommunicated) with Mary as a Catholic monarch. Executing Mary removed this threat.

Why was Mary Queen of Scots executed?

Mary remained a rallying point for discontented Catholics and had a legitimate claim to the English throne. Executing her made it harder for Catholics to plot against Elizabeth in future.

Mary's execution removed this threat to Elizabeth's monarchy. This left Elizabeth without an heir, although by the 1590s many believed this was likely to be Mary's Protestant son, James VI of Scotland.

The execution of Mary Queen of Scots, on 8 February 1587 at Fotheringhay Castle.

Philip II of Spain had a claim to the English throne as the former husband of Mary Tudor. Mary Queen of Scots' death, as a Catholic, may have reinforced his determination to depose Elizabeth.

Now try this

Explain why the execution of Mary Queen of Scots both benefitted and threatened Elizabeth.

Reasons for conflict

The conflict between England and Spain was caused by political, religious and commercial rivalry.

Religious rivalry

Under Mary Tudor, Spain and England were allies. As a Protestant country under Elizabeth I, England's relationship with Spain deteriorated:

- Philip II, backed by the pope, saw Protestantism as a threat to the authority of the Catholic Church.
- Many English Protestants saw Spain and Catholicism as a threat.
- Philip II of Spain became involved in Catholic plots against Elizabeth.

Philip II was married to Elizabeth's half-sister, Mary Tudor. After Mary died, Philip proposed to Elizabeth in 1559, but she declined him because he was Catholic.

Political rivalry

- Rivalry between Spain and England got worse owing to Spanish policy in the Netherlands.
- The Netherlands had been Spanish since the 15th century, but a Protestant revolt was brutally put down by the Duke of Alba in 1567.
- By 1585, following the Treaty of Nonsuch, England was providing assistance to the Dutch rebels. Dutch ships, known as the Sea Beggars, attacked Spanish ships and then were allowed to shelter in English ports.

Turn to page 22 for more on Philip II's involvement in the the Ridolfi plot.

By the 1560s England and Spain were commercial (trade) rivals, competing against each other for access to the markets and resources of the New World, as well as markets in Turkey, Europe, Russia, China and North Africa.

At the same time Spanish control of the New World denied English merchants profit-making opportunities because all trade there had to be licensed by the Spanish government.

Spain conquered Mexico and Peru in the early 1500s. This provided the Spanish government with vast amounts of gold and silver, which were regularly shipped back to Spain. It also gave Spain control over the trade of sugar cane and tobacco.

Commercial rivalry

By Elizabeth's reign, sailors including Sir Francis Drake were journeying great distances on trading voyages to different parts of the world. This boosted commercial rivalry between England and Spain, as English sailors were exploring and trading in areas, such as the New World and the Far East, which the Spanish claimed as their territory.

Commercial rivalry led to conflict when Spanish control of the Netherlands prevented English goods accessing Antwerp and the Scheldt estuary. This reduced English trade with Europe and therefore the profits of English merchants.

Under the Treaty of Tordesillas of 1494, the right to explore and trade in the New World was given to Spain and Portugal. This gave Spain control of trade in the New World. English trade and exploration in the region was seen as a challenge to Spain's dominance there.

English privateering

- By the 1570s English privateers such as Hawkins and Drake were attacking Spanish treasure ships carrying gold and silver across the Atlantic.
- By the 1580s these attacks by privateers were costing Spain hugely – when Drake returned to England after his circumnavigation of the globe, he did so with £400 000 of Spanish treasure.

Typically, private investors, including the queen, provided money and funding to pay for the expeditions and were repaid with a proportion of the looted treasure.

By knighting Drake in 1581, Elizabeth demonstrated her support for English privateers as well as her hostility towards Spain's commercial interests in Europe and the New World.

Philip II viewed Drake and other privateers as pirates who should be removed by war if necessary. This would protect Spain's commercial interests.

See page 9 for more on privateering.

Now try this

Write a paragraph to explain why England's increasing trade activity caused conflict with Spain.

Naval warfare: tactics and technology

England's war with Spain was characterised by **naval** actions including privateering and attacks on Spanish bases.

Naval means relating to a navy or navies (ships).

Attacks on Spanish bases

Privateers attacked Spanish colonies (foreign countries ruled by Spain) and bases in both Europe and the Pacific from the 1560s to the 1580s.

- In 1568 an expedition led by John Hawkins was heavily defeated in the Caribbean. All except two of his ships were destroyed.

- From 1572 to 1573 Francis Drake successfully raided the Spanish colony of Panama, seizing gold and silver.

- During his circumnavigation of the globe (1577–1580), Drake's attacks on Spanish bases in the Pacific and the Canaries resulted in the capture of gold, silver and Spanish coins (pieces of eight or pesos).

- In 1587 Drake attacked Spanish ships at Cadiz in southern Spain. This was his most devastating attack on the Spanish, with 30 Spanish ships destroyed and many captured. This delayed and weakened the Spanish Armada that sailed in 1588.

Drake's own map of the Spanish attack on Cadiz in 1587. The attack became known as 'the singeing of the King of Spain's beard' and delayed the departure of the Spanish Armada.

For more on privateering, see page 29. For more on the Spanish Armada turn to page 31.

English naval tactics and technology

By the 1570s English tactics were starting to change:

- The English had mounted a number of small cannons on their ships, which could be reloaded quickly.

- The plan was to get as close as possible to Spanish vessels and fire devastating rounds of shot (small lead balls) into their ships, causing the wood to splinter and leading to casualties.

- The English had to get close enough to cause damage – but not close enough to allow the Spanish to board their ships.

- Since 1573 English shipyards had produced ships that had full rigging (sails), allowing them to manoeuvre more easily among enemy ships before sinking or disabling them using cannons.

An English galleon. These were superior to Spanish ships because they were swifter and easier to manoeuvre.

Spanish naval tactics

- The Spanish practised a convoy system – with treasure ships travelling in a large group of other ships for protection. For privateers to seize these ships they would have to board them. The Spanish prevented this by sinking the privateers' ships or boarding them.

- To board and capture English ships, the Spanish had to get as close as possible.

- To sink ships, the Spanish ships carried cannons, but these were relatively large and could not easily be reloaded. The Spanish were also unable to sustain their fire against English ships.

Spanish tactics, both against the Dutch and the English, were defensive. They protected treasure ships and escorted troops at sea – so English privateers preferred to attack bases after the treasure had been unloaded.

Now try this

Explain **two** advantages that the English navy had over the Spanish by 1587.

The defeat of the Spanish Armada

The threat posed by the Spanish Armada of 1588 was very real: invasion by a powerful Catholic country and the removal of Elizabeth from power. The Armada was defeated for a number of reasons.

What happened to the Armada of 1588?

Timeline

31 July Battle of Plymouth. Two Spanish ships are captured.

29 July The Armada is spotted in the English Channel.

3–4 August Battle of the Isle of Wight. Spanish ships are outgunned by the English and forced to move further up the channel towards Calais.

8 August Battle of Gravelines. Fireships cause the Spanish to panic. The Spanish fleet never links up with the Duke of Parma and is scattered.

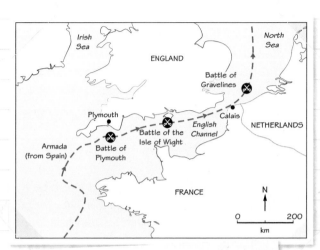

The route of the Spanish Armada, 1588

Communication problems:

- There was no communication between the Duke of Parma and the Duke of Medina-Sidonia.
- There were no deep-water ports. The Dutch rebels still possessed Ostend. This meant the Spanish Armada could not stop at any ports in the Spanish Netherlands, but had to meet up with the Duke of Parma's army at sea after it had embarked on a series of smaller ships. This made communications very difficult.

English ships were better armed and equipped.

In English ships, cannons were mounted on smaller gun carriages than on Spanish ships. This meant they could be reloaded and fired more quickly than the Spanish cannons. This firepower damaged many Spanish ships and undermined their chances of linking up with the Duke of Parma and invading England.

Spanish ships lacked supplies and provisions, including food, for a long voyage.

The Spanish fleet was at sea for 10 weeks and by early August the food had rotted. This damaged Spanish morale and their ability to fight the English.

Reasons for the English victory

The Spanish panicked.

The key turning point seems to have been the Battle of Gravelines, where the English used fireships. Many Spanish captains panicked, cut their anchors and allowed their ships to drift into the North Sea. This meant the Spanish ships were forced to make a dangerous journey around the British Isles, resulting in the loss of ships and crew.

English tactics were superior:

- The English got close enough to the Spanish ships to fire on them, but stayed far enough away to prevent Spanish sailors and soldiers from boarding. This destroyed and damaged a number of Spanish ships while ensuring that English losses were minimal.
- Drake's use of fireships at the Battle of Gravelines was also important as it caused the Spanish to panic.

The weather.

Gale force winds caused most of the destruction to the Spanish ships as they retreated home. Many Spanish ships were destroyed off the west of Ireland.

Fireships were small ships that were set on fire and allowed to drift into the Spanish ships.

Turn to page 30 for more on English and Spanish naval tactics.

Now try this

Explain why English tactics led to the defeat of the Spanish Armada in 1588. Give **at least two** reasons.

Site investigation

You will study **one** particular Elizabethan site in depth. The site will be linked to the rest of your British depth study on Elizabethan England. You will be told which site you are studying, and you will consider a range of information and resources connected with the site. There are seven key aspects about your site (they are numbered below) that you need to consider. You need to learn facts about these key aspects and you need an understanding of the site's historical context.

Context and second order concepts

Consider the wider historical **context**: what's the background to the site? You also need to explore the following second order concepts:

- ✓ **Change** – How has the site changed from earlier periods?

- ✓ **Continuity** – How has the site stayed the same?

- ✓ **Causation** – What caused the site's change or continuity? For example, why were pews added to St Swithin's Church in Bude?

- ✓ **Consequence** – What were the consequences of building the site, for example a theatre in Elizabethan London?

> Look out for links between the key aspects, too!

❶ Location

Make sure you understand your site's **location**: Where was it built? Why was it built there? What do aerial photographs suggest about its location?

❷ Function

Find out about your site's **function**: What was it used for? Did people live there? Was it a religious building? Did it demonstrate the wealth and status of the owner or occupier? Was it used for military or business purposes, or to entertain people?

❸ Structure

What are the key facts about the **structure** of your site? Think about key rooms or areas of the site and where these are located within the site.

> For example, if your site is a house, did it have a Great Hall and how was it used? Did it have a parlour or personal apartments? If your site is a theatre, where are the stage, galleries and stalls?

❹ People

Explore the full range of **people** connected with your site. For example: Who built it? Who lived there? Who may have visited the site? Who worked there, including servants?

> Think about how people lived at the time. How were they governed? What were their beliefs?

❺ Design

- How was the site designed and built?
- What was the style of the **architecture**?

> **Architecture** refers to the design and construction of buildings.

- Does the site show the Elizabethan interest in symmetry (balance) and order?
- How does the site's design reflect Elizabethan culture?

❻ Culture, values and fashions

- How does the site reflect the period?
- How does it reflect Elizabethan social order, status and fashions?
- For example, if your site is a house, did the residents live on the upper floors and the servants in the basement?
- For example, if your site is a theatre, did the wealthy sit in special galleries or on stage?

❼ Important events and developments

Think about what was happening in England at the time and how your site links in with key events: for example, Elizabeth's religious settlement or developments in the theatre.

Now try this

Write down **one** fact about the site you are studying for each of the seven key headings above.

📍 Site investigation | Sample site: Speke Hall 1

Have a look at the seven key aspects on page 32. This page and the next give you examples of each aspect for one sample site as well as examples of change, continuity, causation and consequence.

Watch out: you will not be considering Speke Hall in your exam, so you don't need to learn these facts. You will need to make notes on the seven aspects for **your** selected site.

Context

Speke Hall. Today, it is run by the National Trust.

- Built by the Norris family between 1530 and 1598.
- A typical Elizabethan oak-framed house.
- The Norris family were Catholics, so did not support Elizabeth's religious settlement of 1559. They faced growing fines for being recusants.

See page 19 for details of the Elizabethan religious settlement of 1559. To remind yourself about recusants, turn to page 21.

① Location

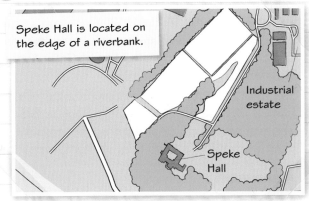

Speke Hall is located on the edge of a riverbank.

Industrial estate

Speke Hall

- Located near Liverpool airport, close to the Mersey Estuary.
- Built on the site of an old medieval manor house.
- Located close to the river and could be seen from the riverbank, so advertising the wealth and status of the Norris family.

② Function

Continuity Speke Hall was a place of residence for the Norris family between the reigns of Henry VIII and Charles II (1509–1685).

In the Great Hall guests were entertained and business conducted. It was also a dining room.

Change After the religious settlement of 1559, the house was probably used to hide priests and conduct secret Catholic Masses.

A **peephole** allowed occupants to see who was coming. An **eavesdrop** was a hole that allowed servants to listen in on conversations.

Consequence The Norris family may have avoided entertaining guests from outside the local area to avoid being unmasked as Catholics (punishments included death).

③ Structure

The foundations were made of red sandstone, with **wattle and daub** used to fill in the gaps between the timber frames to make walls.

Wattle and daub is a material that was used to make walls during the Elizabethan period.

Consequence The combination of sandstone, timber frame and glass, as well as an ornamental moat, reflected the family's wealth and importance.

Causation The need for the Norris family to conceal their Catholic faith led to various security measures in the house, such as **priest's holes**, **peepholes** and **eavesdrops**.

Consequence There were no significant changes to the house's layout after it was completed in 1598 because the family couldn't afford it owing to high recusancy fines.

Now try this

Describe **two** features of Speke Hall that demonstrate that the occupiers of the house were Catholic.

Site investigation — Sample site: Speke Hall 2

Make sure you have revised pages 32 and 33 before looking at this page.

4 People

The Norris family were part of the gentry class in Elizabethan England.

See page 9 for more on the gentry.

Continuity The family owned Speke Hall from the late 14th to early 18th centuries.

Continuity Like many landowners in north-west England, the family remained loyal Catholics during Elizabeth's reign.

The family's servants – including cooks, those who looked after horses, gardeners, launderers (those who washed clothes) and personal servants – were most probably Catholic too, as north-west England was a strongly Catholic area.

Consequence The family's failure to attend Church of England services meant they lost influence at court.

Wooden relief carving from Speke Hall, showing the many children of the Norris family

5 Design

The North Range was built in 1598 and the South Wing extended between 1540 and 1570. This meant family members slept in their own rooms and enjoyed some privacy.

The use of glass, which included the Norris coat of arms and those of related families, advertised the family's status and wealth.

The front of Speke Hall, showing the sandstone foundations, black timber frame and wattle and daub, characteristic of Elizabethan manor houses.

Change Gardens around the site were added in the 19th century.

6 Culture, values and fashions

Continuity The Norris family's status was determined by the family coat of arms with the motto 'feythfully serve'.

Family coats of arms showed off the importance of the family as members of the gentry, allowing them to socialise and arrange marriages with similar families.

As members of the gentry, the Norris family:

- would have followed Tudor fashions, wearing clothes that reflected their social position, such as gilt or velvet
- were expected to eat well and entertain other members of the gentry at banquets with imported sweet wines.

See page 8 for more on Elizabethan fashions and the Sumptuary Laws.

7 Important events and developments

Causation The Elizabethan religious settlement made the Church in England Protestant.

See page 19 for details of the Elizabethan religious settlement.

Causation There was growing suspicion of Catholics during Elizabeth's reign, in part due to Catholic missionaries as well as plots against her.

Turn to pages 20 and 22–23 for more on the Northern Rebellion, Catholic missionaries and Catholic plots during Elizabeth's reign.

Consequence The Norris family had to be secretive about their religion.

See page 33 for more on peepholes, priest's holes and eavesdrops at Speke Hall.

Now try this

Give **two** facts about Speke Hall that show that Tudor houses were built to demonstrate the importance of their owners.

⊙ Site investigation Sample site: Blackfriars Theatre 1

Remind yourself of the seven key aspects on page 32. This page and the next give examples of each aspect for a second sample site as well as examples of change, continuity, causation and consequence.

Watch out: you will not write about Blackfriars Theatre in your exam, so you don't need to learn these facts. You do need to make notes on the seven aspects for **your** selected site.

Context

Blackfriars Theatre in the City of London was built on the site of the old Blackfriars monastery, first constructed in 1278.

Change In 1538 under Henry VIII, Blackfriars monastery was dissolved and various buildings were sold.

The first, smaller theatre (the old theatre) was based in the old refectory (dining area) of the monastery. It staged plays by boy actors from 1576 to 1584.

The second, very spacious theatre (the new theatre) dates from the purchase of the upper part of the monastery by James Burbage in 1596.

Change Plays by Elizabethan playwrights such as William Shakespeare, Christopher Marlowe and Ben Jonson became increasingly popular in London.

❶ Location

- Found near the banks of the River Thames.
- Within the walled City of London, where many of the nobility lived.
- Close to other Elizabethan theatres south of the River Thames – the Swan, the Globe, the Bear Garden and the Rose.

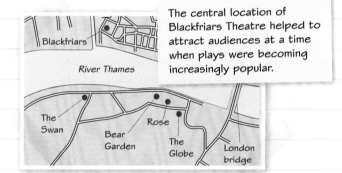

The central location of Blackfriars Theatre helped to attract audiences at a time when plays were becoming increasingly popular.

❷ Function

Continuity The main function of the two theatres was to perform plays for paying audiences.

Both theatres paid for theatrical companies, such as Oxford's Boys, and famous actors, including Nathaniel Field, to perform. They recovered this money by charging audience admission to see the plays. The owners could make £13.00 from a single performance – a large sum at the time.

Change From 1576 onwards Richard Farrant staged plays in a converted refectory for paying audiences. Admission cost 4 pence, then a considerable sum, so plays were mostly attended by wealthier classes.

❸ Structure

Continuity Both theatres were part of the original monastic buildings, built from stone blocks approximately three feet wide.

The smaller theatre was based in an upper room, about 46 feet (14 metres) long and 25 feet (8 metres) wide.

The larger theatre was a roofed theatre around 100 feet (30 metres) long and 50 feet (15 metres) wide, with high ceilings. James Burbage built two galleries in the space, to increase audience numbers.

Change The second Blackfriars theatre was a roofed theatre built in 1596. It housed plays for larger audiences of 600 to 1000.

Now try this

Explain **one** way in which the function of Blackfriars Theatre changed during Elizabeth's reign.

Site investigation Sample site: Blackfriars Theatre 2

Make sure you revise pages 32 and 35 before looking at this page.

4 People

Change In 1576 part of the old monastery was leased to Richard Farrant, Master of the Children of the Chapel Royal, who put on plays by boy actors there.

Change James Burbage built the second (new) theatre in 1596. Burbage was an actor, builder and theatre owner.

After his father's death, Richard Burbage leased the theatre to Henry Evans in 1600. Richard Burbage (1567–1619) is considered the first great actor of English theatre.

The audience in the original theatre was made up of merchants and members of the gentry, who could afford the fees for private performances.

Larger audiences attended the second theatre, although only the rich could afford it.

Plays by leading playwrights, such as Thomas Middleton, Ben Jonson, George Chapman and John Marston, were incredibly popular.

5 Design

- At least two and possibly three galleries.
- A number of stage boxes.
- As many as ten spectators may have sat on or close to the stage during performances.

The second (new) Blackfriars Theatre may have looked like this.

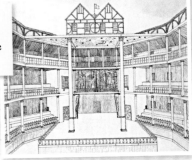

Change Burbage added trap doors, wires and belts, to hang props and lower actors. Blackfriars Theatre was also among the first in England to use artificial lighting and to play music between acts.

6 Culture, values and fashions

- All actors were male. Boys played all the female parts, often wearing wigs.
- Costumes reflected the characters' status. Actors playing gentry, nobility or monarchs had to invest in costumes that reflected their status, which was very expensive.
- Actors painted their faces for the performance.
- Many plays reflected the vulgar humour of Elizabethan society and pushed the boundaries of what was acceptable. Audiences enjoyed the plays' vulgarity as well as their comedy.
- The plays were also popular because they addressed the interests of Elizabethan society, including history (*Henry V*, *Julius Caesar*) and witchcraft (*Macbeth*).
- Such plays were often condemned by Puritans.
- Public galleries allowed the wealthier members of society to be seen by others.

7 Important events and developments

Causation Plays poked fun at leading figures in late Elizabethan society, were often violent and included sexual content.

Consequence In 1596 the City of London's authorities responded to complaints by banning plays and all theatres, which had to move south of the River Thames.

Change From 1600, Henry Evans staged plays at the new Blackfriars Theatre.

Continuity From 1610 until 1642, the Blackfriars Theatre was celebrated for its innovative drama by talented playwrights.

Causation When the English Civil War started in 1642, the Blackfriars Theatre closed.

Consequence The Blackfriars Theatre fell into disrepair and was demolished in 1655.

Now try this

Give **two** ways in which the culture, values and fashions of the people connected with Blackfriars Theatre are reflected in its design and use.

Exam overview

This page introduces you to the main features and requirements of the Paper 2 Section B exam paper for Elizabethan England, c1568–1603.

About Paper 2

- Paper 2 is for both your thematic study and your British depth study.

- Section B of the paper will be on your British depth study. Elizabethan England, c1568–1603 is one of the depth study options and includes the historic environment.

- Section B will include questions about other British depth study options. You should **only** answer the questions about Elizabethan England, c1568–1603.

- You will receive two documents: a question paper that will contain the questions and interpretations, and an answer booklet.

The Paper 2 exam lasts for 1 hour 45 minutes (105 minutes). There are 84 marks in total: 40 marks, plus 4 marks for spelling, punctuation and grammar, for Section A; **40 marks for Section B.** You should spend approximately 50 minutes on Section A and **50 minutes on Section B**, with 5 minutes to check your answers.

Here we are focusing on Section B and your British depth study. However, the same exam paper will also include Section A, where you will answer questions on your thematic study.

The questions

The questions for Paper 2 Section B will always follow this pattern:

You can see examples of all four questions on pages 40–44 and in the practice questions on pages 45–55.

Question 13

How convincing is **Interpretation C** about …?
Explain your answer using Interpretation C and your contextual knowledge.   **(8 marks)**

Question 13 targets AO4. AO4 is about analysing, **evaluating** and making **substantiated judgements**. Spend about 10 minutes on this question, which is about **analysing and evaluating an interpretation**.

Question 14

Explain what was important about …   **(8 marks)**

Question 14 targets both AO1 and AO2. AO1 is about showing your **knowledge** and **understanding** of the key features and characteristics of the topic. AO2 is about **explaining** and **analysing** historical events using second order concepts such as causation, consequence, change, continuity, similarity and difference. Spend about 10 minutes on this question, which focuses on **explaining why** an issue or event was important.

Question 15

Write an account …   **(8 marks)**

Question 15 also targets AO1 and AO2. Spend about 10 minutes on this question, which requires you to write a **narrative account**.

Question 16

[Statement]
How far does a study of [historic site] support this statement?
Explain your answer.
You should refer to [historic site] and your contextual knowledge.   **(16 marks)**

Question 16 also targets AO1 and AO2. Spend about 20 minutes on this question, which requires you to make a **judgement** in an **extended response about the historic environment site you have studied**.

Interpretation skills

Question 13 on your exam paper will ask you to analyse, evaluate and make judgements about interpretations.

What is an interpretation?

For the first question in the exam paper you will be asked to study an **interpretation** and comment on how convincing it is.

Interpretations are compiled after the time period or event they describe. An interpretation can be text:

✓ an account written by a historian

✓ a poem

✓ a work of fiction.

It might also be an image:

✓ a reconstructive drawing

✓ a diagram

✓ a poster

✓ an advertisement

✓ a painting.

All interpretations will contain people's views and opinions.

Analysing interpretations

When analysing interpretations, you need to try to work out the **message** of the interpretation. You then need to evaluate the interpretation for question 13 on your exam paper, which asks you **how convincing** the interpretation is.

Convincing means historically convincing. You need to compare the interpretation to your knowledge of the period. Does it fit with what you know? If you were to go to Elizabethan England, how close is it to what you would see?

Contextual knowledge

Question 13 will ask you to explain your answer using the interpretation and your **contextual knowledge**. This means that you need to think about what you know about the event or development. Does it support or contradict the message of the interpretation? Only use knowledge that's relevant to the topic in the question and is linked to what is discussed or shown in the interpretation itself.

Provenance

Before the interpretation in the exam paper you will be given several lines of **provenance** (authorship). This is likely to include some details about the author and their work or experiences, and when their work was published.

You should use the information in the provenance to help you establish the **purpose** of the interpretation. However, you do not need to evaluate the provenance itself in the exam.

Hints and tips for analysing and evaluating interpretations

What's the focus?	What is shown/described?
Interpretations can approach a topic from very specific angles. Sometimes, historians set out to look at one aspect specifically, whereas others may want to look at related issues in a broader sense. An artist might want to convey a sense of drama rather than focus on accuracy. Remember, you do not need to discuss what is **not** shown. You will only get credit for discussing what **is** shown.	A useful mnemonic here is **PEA**: ✓ **People:** Who is shown/described in the interpretation? Is the picture or description convincing? Why or why not? ✓ **Environment:** Where is the interpretation set? Is it accurate? Why or why not? ✓ **Activity:** What is happening in the interpretation? Is it an accurate representation? Was this a normal occurrence or not?

Interpretation C

This interpretation is referred to in the worked example on page 40.

SECTION B

Elizabethan England, c1568–1603

Use **Interpretation C t**o answer question 13 on page 40.

Interpretation C: This is an interpretation of Robert Devereux, Earl of Essex. It depicts Devereux threatening to draw his sword on the queen following a dispute in 1598. The picture is from a children's history book written in the 1970s.

You will be given some information about the subject of the interpretation. In this case, you are told that the interpretation shows Robert Devereux threatening Elizabeth I after an argument in 1598.

You will be given short details on where the interpretation comes from. In this case, you are told the type of book and when it was written.

Annotate the interpretation with your ideas. If the interpretation is an image, such as this one, think about the details you can see. If the interpretation is a text extract, underline or highlight any important words or phrases and annotate them.

Question 13: Evaluating interpretations

Question 13 on your exam paper will ask you to evaluate how convincing an interpretation is in relation to a particular aspect of the topic. There are 8 marks available for this question.

Worked example

 Links   You can revise the rebellion of Robert Devereux, Earl of Essex, on page 7.

How convincing is **Interpretation C** on page 39 as a depiction of the relationship between Robert Devereux, Earl of Essex, and Queen Elizabeth?

Explain your answer using **Interpretation C** and your contextual knowledge.   **(8 marks)**

Evaluating an interpretation

✓ Consider **how convincing** (believable) the image or text is – is it a good interpretation of what actually happened or what the event would have been like?

✓ Think about whether it matches your **contextual knowledge** – what you know about the topic.

✓ Comment on **more than one aspect** (part) of the interpretation and link it up with your own knowledge.

✓ **Explain** your ideas by giving reasons for the points you make.

✓ Finish with a **conclusion** summarising how convincing the interpretation is.

Sample answer

Interpretation C is a convincing picture of the relationship between the queen and Devereux. Robert Devereux, the Earl of Essex, did draw his sword on the queen after she slapped him in the face and told him to 'go and be hanged'. The Earl of Essex, a leading courtier, would have behaved like this when his pride was hurt in this way.

 Start with a clear introduction, stating whether or not you think the interpretation is convincing.

Comment on **more than one aspect** of the interpretation. Here the student focuses only on Devereux drawing his sword – they do not explore why this happened.

Improved answer

In many ways Interpretation C is a convincing portrayal of the relationship between Elizabeth and Devereux. The queen did box Robert Devereux, the Earl of Essex, on the ears and told him to 'go and be hanged'. This happened after William Knollys, and not Devereux, was made Lord Lieutenant of Ireland. Essex did respond by drawing his sword.

The detail in the scene is also convincing as it shows the queen and the courtiers dressed in the style of the period.

Furthermore, the interpretation is convincing in how it shows Devereux being restrained. This highlights how his relationship with the queen had worsened owing to rivalries at court between himself, Robert Cecil and others, as well as Essex's failures in dealing with the Spanish. Devereux was no longer the queen's favourite and this comes out in the interpretation.

However, the depiction is not completely convincing as it suggests that the relationship between the queen and Devereux had completely collapsed. This was not the case. Elizabeth was still prepared to send Essex to Ireland to crush a rebellion there. It was his failure to achieve this and the rebellion of 1601 that fatally damaged their relationship, not the event depicted in the interpretation.

Identify and comment on **more than one aspect** of the interpretation. Here, the student refers to Devereux drawing his sword as well as the roles of the queen and court rivalry. Contextual knowledge (Essex's failure with the Spanish, his inability to crush the Irish revolt and his rebellion of 1601) is also used to support the answer.

 Remember **PEA**. Start with the **people**. Your answer should point out detail and then link it to specific knowledge of the period.

 Move on to the **environment**. Focus on a detail and explain why it is or is not convincing by contrasting it with contextual knowledge.

 Then look at **activity**. Describe what is happening in the picture and why it is convincing.

Question 14:
Explaining importance

Question 14 on your exam paper is about explaining importance: explaining the significance of an event by referring to its consequences. There are 8 marks available for this question.

Worked example

Explain what was important about the execution of Mary Queen of Scots in 1587 for Elizabethan England. **(8 marks)**

Sample answer

The execution of Mary Queen of Scots was important because it removed a potential rival to Elizabeth's throne. This made rebellion and plotting harder, as there was no longer someone else to put on the throne. This made it less likely that Catholic plots and rebellions such as the Northern Rebellion of 1569–1570 and the Babington plot of 1586 would happen again.

Refer to two or more **consequences** of the issue or event given in the question. This response really only explains one consequence of the execution of Mary Queen of Scots. The student needs to include more detailed explanation – for example, why was the execution important in terms of England's relationship with Catholic France and Spain?

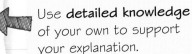 **Links** Look back at pages 26–28 to revise the events leading up to the execution of Mary Queen of Scots.

How to explain importance

To answer this question, you need to say **how or why** something was **important**. You should:

✓ refer to two or more **consequences** of the issue or event given in the question – here the execution of Mary Queen of Scots

✓ use your **own knowledge** of the period

✓ give **evidence and examples** to support and justify the points you make

✓ use second order concepts in your explanation. A good way to do this is to use sentence starters like 'One reason for this was …' or 'This was important because …'.

Improved answer

The execution of Mary Queen of Scots was important because it removed a potential rival to Elizabeth's throne, angered Spain and set a dangerous precedent as a monarch had been executed.

Executing Mary Queen of Scots made it harder for Elizabeth's subjects to rebel against her, as there was no longer an alternative monarch to replace her. This made Catholic plots and rebellions such as the Northern Rebellion of 1569–1570 and the Babington plot of 1586 less likely to succeed.

Mary's execution also provoked Spain and potentially France as well. France and Spain were Catholic, and Mary had been married to the French king, Francis II. More importantly, Mary's claim to the English throne passed to Philip II of Spain at Mary's request and as a result of his previous marriage to Mary Tudor. If Philip, backed by the pope, attacked England in an attempt to overthrow Elizabeth, France would be unlikely to offer help – even though Spain was a rival. Mary's execution meant the commercial and religious rivalry between England and Spain became outright war.

Mary's execution also set a dangerous precedent: Elizabeth had signed the death warrant of another monarch. This made it easier for both Philip II and the pope to justify Elizabeth's removal and execution through invasion. This led directly to the formation of the Spanish Armada in 1588.

Start by signposting your answer and highlighting the points that will be covered.

Use **detailed knowledge** of your own to support your explanation.

Remember to include detailed analysis and link your points together. Here, the student builds on the previous paragraph.

 Make sure your answer refers to the **historical context** and refers to **consequences**.

Question 15: Narrative account

Question 15 on your exam paper requires you to write a narrative account analysing how and why a historical event happened. There are 8 marks available for this question.

Worked example

🔗 **Links** Turn to page 7 for more on Essex's rebellion.

Write an account of the ways in which Essex's rebellion affected Elizabethan England.   **(8 marks)**

Sample answer

The Essex rebellion occurred when Robert Devereux, Earl of Essex, gathered 300 supporters at Essex House, which he had fortified. The rebels planned to march to Paul's Cross and persuade people to join them.

Before the rebellion began the Lord Chancellor and other Royal Officers visited Essex, who imprisoned them. Essex then rode into London asking people to arm themselves and follow him.

This answer contains good subject knowledge but is really only narrative that describes the rebellion, which isn't asked for. The student needs to explore not only the events of the rebellion but also its impact on Elizabethan England.

What is a narrative account?

A **narrative account** is not simply a description of what happened. To write a successful narrative account you need to:

☑ think about **key elements** of the event and how they were **connected**

☑ consider what the account needs to do – you may need to think about cause, change, continuity and/or consequence

☑ use your own knowledge of the period

☑ structure your narrative logically, so it has a clear order.

Improved answer

The Essex rebellion affected Elizabethan England because it ended the rivalries that existed in the late Elizabethan court.

During the 1590s there were two key groups at court, one centred on Robert Cecil, Earl of Salisbury, the other centred on Robert Devereux, Earl of Essex. These groups fell out over the situation in Ireland, when Essex was originally overlooked for the position of Lord Lieutenant there and was then accused of failing to put down the rebellion there.

The failure of Essex's rebellion was important because it ended these divisions and meant that Robert Cecil and his supporters went on to control the government for the rest of Elizabeth's reign.

Essex's failure and execution also showed that there were limits on the powers of the nobility. They could no longer hope to increase their power by rebelling against the government. This meant that Elizabeth's government was stronger by the end of her reign, as it was less vulnerable to plots and rebellions.

Make sure you set your knowledge in the broader **historical context**.

Make sure you explain the **effect** of the changes, not just the changes. Here the student successfully explains how Essex's loss of favour at court and the impact of his failure in Ireland led to the rebellion.

Link your paragraphs together to show you are structuring your answer logically. Here the student links the Essex rebellion to the previous paragraph, showing a detailed understanding of the event.

The answer gives detailed factual information and also shows how the rebellion affected Elizabethan England.

Question 16:
Historic environment 1

On your exam paper, the last question for Section B on your British depth study of Elizabethan England will focus on the historic environment. You will be given a statement and asked **how far** a study of your historical site supports the statement. There are 16 marks available for this question.

Worked example

'The main change that the construction of theatres demonstrated was the growing appeal of popular plays in Elizabethan England.'

How far does a study of Blackfriars Theatre support this statement?

Explain your answer.

You should refer to Blackfriars Theatre and your contextual knowledge.   **(16 marks)**

Watch out: You will not be considering Blackfriars Theatre in your exam. You will need to answer a similar question based on the site you have studied.

Remember the **seven key aspects: location; function; structure; people; design; culture, values and fashions; and important events and developments**. Use these aspects to help structure your answer.

Compare the answer extract below with an improved version on the next page.

Links See pages 35 and 36 to revise Blackfriars Theatre.

'How far ...' questions

This extended answer question is asking you to balance **evidence** to come up with an argument – a **line of reasoning**. You need to:

- ✓ describe **aspects**/features of the historical site that support the statement in the question, giving reasons to explain why they support the statement

- ✓ do the same for any aspects/features of the site that either contradict the statement or that you would expect to see in a typical site but are missing from this one

- ✓ develop a **sustained** line of reasoning – 'sustained' means you need to present a clear, logical argument **throughout your answer**

- ✓ use **evidence** from your site **study** and from the **wider historical context**

- ✓ make a **judgement** – you need to decide 'how far' by reaching a conclusion based on the facts and reasoning in your answer.

Sample extract

The location of both Blackfriars Theatres shows the growing popularity of plays in England. The theatres were located close to the walled city of London to attract audiences to plays written by Shakespeare, Marlowe, Jonson and others.

The function of the theatres also shows the growing appeal of plays. Both Richard Farrant, who set up the first theatre, and James Burbage hoped to profit by charging people to see the plays.

The structure of the theatre also shows their growing popularity. Both theatres constructed at Blackfriars made use of professional players. It was hoped this would attract more people.

The design of the second theatre, which opened in 1600, also shows this. Contemporary accounts suggest it could hold audiences of between 600 and 1000 people.

In a full answer, you should begin with a **short introduction** to signpost your argument

Keep your points **relevant** – here, the point about function is accurate, but not really relevant.

Give a clear answer to the 'how far' part of the question, and give examples of other changes. These points are missing here.

Use key phrases like 'on the other hand' or 'however', especially when you make a new point.

In a full answer, you should end with a **conclusion** summarising your judgement about **how far** a study of the site supports the statement in the question.

Question 16:
Historic environment 2

This page has an improved version of the answer extract given on the previous page.

Wider historical context

The historic environment question asks you to use both your knowledge of the site and your **contextual knowledge**. You will need to consider the question from two angles:

 Think about what you know about the topic given in the question – is there evidence for this at the site? For example, if your site is a theatre, how many of the main features does it have?

 Think about the main features of the site – how do they link to the historical period? For example, if your site is a theatre, the presence of galleries is evidence that wealthier Elizabethans attended plays.

Improved extract

The construction of theatres demonstrated the growing popularity of English plays. However, it also led to other changes, including the fact that theatres were increasingly important for the social lives of wealthy people.

Start your answer with a **short, clear introduction**, which shows you are considering both sides of the issue.

The construction of theatres suggests that plays were growing in popularity in Elizabethan England. The construction of two theatres at Blackfriars, an old Dominican priory, close to the City of London, in 1576 and 1600, suggests there was a growing appetite among ordinary people for plays such as those written by Jonson, Marlow and Shakespeare.

Use **evidence** from your site study to support the **judgement** you make about the statement in the question. Here, the student is using evidence from their knowledge of the **historical context**, and then moves on to give specific **examples from the site**.

This is reinforced by the design of the second Blackfriars Theatre, which contemporary accounts indicate could house between 600 and 1000 people. This suggests large numbers of Elizabethans went to see popular plays. Furthermore, the designer of the second Blackfriars Theatre, James Burbage, was an actor, builder and theatre owner involved with theatre companies. This supports the argument that the theatre was a business designed to satisfy the growing popularity of plays in Elizabethan England.

Don't only refer to the site you have studied. You also need to refer to the **wider historical context**: the events going on in the background. This answer refers to the plays of Jonson, Marlowe and Shakespeare.

However, other changes were also demonstrated by the construction of theatres in Elizabethan England. Theatres became increasingly popular in the social lives of members of the nobility, gentry and merchant classes, who liked to be seen in the theatre. This is shown by the design of the second Blackfriars Theatre, which allowed wealthy people to sit in galleries and even on the stage, where plays were performed around them. Members of the nobility such as the Earl of Leicester were keen to sponsor companies of theatrical players. This again shows the growing importance of the theatres in enhancing the wealth and status of those at the top of society.

Using a word such as 'however' signposts that you are moving on to consider the other side of the argument. This shows that you are following a **sustained line of reasoning**.

Make sure all your points are relevant to the question. Each point should answer the question about **how far** the popularity of plays influenced the construction of Elizabethan theatres. Give specific **examples from the site** you are studying throughout your answer.

In your full answer, you should end with a **conclusion** summing up your judgement.

Practice

You will need to refer to the interpretation below in your answer to question 13 on page 46.

SECTION B

Elizabethan England, c1568–1603

Answer **all four questions** on pages 46 to 52.

Use **Interpretation C t**o answer question 13 on page 46.

Interpretation C: An interpretation of Mary Queen of Scots. It portrays her role in the Babington plot of 1586. The text is from a history book written by the novelist and historian, Peter Ackroyd, in 2012.

> A conspiracy was even then being formed against her [Elizabeth], guided by a Jesuit priest John Ballard, and by Mary's agent in Paris. They had recruited a rich young Catholic, Anthony Babington, and he had in turn recruited six courtiers who at the appropriate moment would rise up and assassinate Elizabeth.

Practice

Put your skills and knowledge into practice with the following question. You will need to refer to Interpretation C on page 45 in your answer.

13 How convincing is **Interpretation C** about the threat posed by Mary Queen of Scots?

Explain your answer using **Interpretation C** and your contextual knowledge.

(8 marks)

Guided The interpretation is convincing about the threat

posed by Mary Queen of Scots because it suggests she

was involved in a plot to assassinate Queen Elizabeth.

....

....

....

....

....

....

....

....

....

....

....

....

....

....

....

....

....

....

....

....

....

....

....

....

You have 1 hour 45 minutes for the **whole** of Paper 2, which means you have about **50 minutes** for Section B. In the exam, remember to leave 5 minutes or so to check your work when you've finished both Sections A and B.

Spend about 10 minutes on this answer.

⚲ **Links** You can revise Mary Queen of Scots on pages 26–28.

You need to discuss the content of the interpretation in context – you **must** use your own **contextual knowledge** about the threat Mary posed to Elizabeth in your answer.

Pick out **at least two key details** from the interpretation: for example, the conspiracy, the role of Babington and the Catholic Church, the assassination of the queen.

Do these key details agree with your contextual knowledge or contradict it?

Think about the way in which Walsingham monitored and deciphered Mary's correspondence in order to reduce the threat to Elizabeth and her government. Also think about Mary's involvement in other plots, including the Ridolfi and Throckmorton plots.

Practice

Use this page to continue your answer to question 13.

....

....

....

....

....

....

....

....

....

....

....

....

....

....

....

⬅ Remember, you do not need to discuss what is **not** present in the interpretation. Focus on what is there, comment on **at least two** aspects and explain whether or not they fit with your knowledge.

⬅ Finish your answer with a clear **conclusion** – it need not be long – setting out how convincing the interpretation is.

Practice

Put your skills and knowledge into practice with the following question.

14 Explain what was important about the problem of Puritanism in Elizabethan England.

(8 marks)

Guided Puritanism posed a major problem for Elizabeth's government, as many Puritans did not accept the religious settlement of 1559.

....

....

....

....

....

....

....

....

....

....

....

....

....

....

....

....

....

....

....

....

....

 This question is asking you to say **how or why** something is **important**.

 Spend about 10 minutes on this answer.

Remember, this question asks you to explain the importance of the **consequences** of Puritanism using your own knowledge of the period.

 Links You can revise Puritanism on pages 24 and 25.

 You need to look at the attitude of many Puritans to Elizabeth's religious settlement. Did they fully support it? Did they accept Elizabeth's authority as Head of the Church in England? What was their attitude towards vestments and worship in churches?

 Think about the role of Puritans in Parliament, especially those who were critical of Elizabeth's government.

 Did Puritans encourage people to oppose the government and even rebel? You could refer to Puritan printing presses and the Martin Marprelate tracts.

Practice

Use this page to continue your answer to question 14.

....

....

....

....

....

....

....

....

....

....

....

....

....

⬅ Did some archbishops, especially Grindal, actually encourage Puritanism?

⬅ Remember to use your **own knowledge** and back up your points with **evidence** and **examples**.

Practice

Put your skills and knowledge into practice with the following question.

15 Write an account of the ways in which the Babington plot affected Elizabethan England.

(8 marks)

Guided The Babington plot affected Elizabethan England

because it demonstrated the determination of Catholic

plotters to overthrow Elizabeth

....

....

....

....

....

....

....

....

....

....

....

....

....

....

....

....

....

....

....

Remember that this question asks you to write a narrative account – you need to explain why or how something happened. You will need a clear **structure** to your answer, and you need to back up your argument with **evidence** from **your knowledge** of the Babington plot as well as its impact.

Spend about 10 minutes on this answer.

Links You can revise the Babington plot on page 23.

Think about the **key elements** of the plot and how they are connected. What happened? Who was involved? What were the motives of the plotters? How was the plot prevented?

What were the **consequences** of the plot?
• How did it increase fears of Catholicism in England, so resulting in greater persecution of Catholics?
• How did it lead to the execution of Mary Queen of Scots, setting the scene for the launching of the Spanish Armada in 1588?

Practice

Use this page to continue your answer to question 15.

....

....

....

....

....

....

....

....

....

....

....

....

....

....

Remember to signpost your argument with phrases such as 'However …' and 'As a result …'.

Practice

Put your skills and knowledge into practice with the following question.

Watch out: In the exam you **must** answer on the Elizabethan site you have studied. You will **not** be given a choice of question in the exam.

This is a **how far** question so you need to come up with a balanced response: ideas and evidence about the site that support the statement as well as points that do not.

Choose **either** the Elizabethan site you have studied **or** one of the sites on pages 33–36.

Answer **one** of the following questions.

Remember that for this question on the historic environment you need to **make a judgement** and present a **sustained line of reasoning**.

16a. 'The main change that Elizabethan manor houses demonstrated was the growing power of the gentry.'

How far does a study of your chosen site support this statement?

Explain your answer.

You should refer to your chosen site and your contextual knowledge.

(16 marks)

🔗 **Links** If your site is a manor house, look at this question. You could answer this practice question using the information about Speke Hall on pages 33 and 34.

16b. 'The main change that the design of theatres demonstrated was the growing appeal of popular plays in Elizabethan England.'

How far does a study of your chosen site support this statement?

Explain your answer.

You should refer to your chosen site and your contextual knowledge.

(16 marks)

🔗 **Links** If your site is a theatre, look at this question. You could answer this practice question using the information about Blackfriars Theatre on pages 35 and 36.

16c. 'The main change to churches brought about by Elizabeth's religious settlement was decorative.'

How far does a study of your chosen site support this statement?

Explain your answer.

You should refer to your chosen site and your contextual knowledge.

(16 marks)

If your site is a church, consider this question.

16d. 'The main change to many English towns and cities during Elizabeth's reign was the growing power and influence of the commercial classes.'

How far does a study of your chosen site support this statement?

Explain your answer.

You should refer to your chosen site and your contextual knowledge.

(16 marks)

If your site is a building in a town or city, such as a town hall or an inn, consider this question.

Turn over to start your answer.

Practice

Use this page to start your answer to question 16.

....
....
....
....
....
....
....
....
....
....
....
....
....
....
....
....
....
....
....
....
....
....
....
....
....
....
....
....

← Make sure you **consider all key aspects** of the site: location; function; structure; people; design; culture, values and fashions; important events and developments.

← It is a good idea to **signpost your answer** by beginning each paragraph with a clear statement to give the reader an idea of how the answer will develop. For example, 'There are many ways that the design of Blackfriars Theatre demonstrates the growing appeal of popular plays in Elizabethan England ...' and 'However, there were other changes involving theatres, such as ...'. This will make your answer easier to write and will also make it easier to understand.

Practice

Use this page to continue your answer to question 16.

....

....

....

....

....

....

....

....

....

....

....

....

....

....

....

....

....

....

....

....

....

....

....

....

....

....

....

....

....

....

Make sure that you **discuss more than one aspect** of the site in your answer.

Don't forget the **historical context**. What else was happening at the time? What effect did this have?

Practice

Use this page to continue your answer to question 16.

....

....

....

....

....

....

....

....

....

....

....

....

....

....

....

....

....

....

....

....

← Remember to finish your answer with a clear **conclusion**. Your conclusion should refer to the question and sum up the judgement discussed in your answer. For example: 'A study of Blackfriars Theatre mainly supports the statement that the main change demonstrated by the design of theatres was the growing appeal of popular plays.'

ANSWERS

SUBJECT CONTENT

Elizabeth's court and Parliament

1. Elizabeth's background and character

Any **two** from:
*   Elizabeth was confident and charismatic, which allowed her to win over her subjects and command support in Parliament.
*   Elizabeth was well educated. She spoke Latin, Greek, French and Italian. This enabled her to communicate with foreign diplomats and ambassadors.
*   Elizabeth had an excellent grasp of politics, as she understood the interests and ambitions of her subjects.
*   Although Elizabeth was Protestant, the number of Protestants in England was growing, and this strengthened her position as queen. This meant Elizabeth could claim Divine Right, the idea that God had appointed her as queen, with increasing confidence.
*   When her sister Mary Tudor was queen, Elizabeth was accused of treason and spent time in the Tower under the threat of execution. Elizabeth was tough enough to cope with the pressures of being queen.

2. Court life

Any **two** from:
*   The court often met at one of Elizabeth's many palaces including Greenwich and Hampton Court. The court also moved around the country in Royal Progresses, staying at the country houses of members of the nobility who were required to bear the cost of entertaining the queen and her courtiers. This included providing hospitality as well as gifts for the queen herself.
*   There was a strict dress code. Courtiers were allowed and expected to wear expensive clothes including cloths of gold, silver and dyed velvet, as well as ruffs, which expanded in size over the course of Elizabeth's reign. Attending court could therefore be an expensive business.
*   Courtiers could use their presence at the court to try to influence the queen. This meant that they might benefit from royal patronage, for example by the queen granting them lands, jobs or titles, which would increase their income.
*   The court involved up to 2000 people, and many of these were employed as servants to protect and provide for the court. Many of these servants accompanied the court on a Royal Progress.

3. Elizabeth's ministers

Cecil is on the left and Walsingham on the right. The image suggests that Walsingham and Cecil were important because of their closeness to the queen. This suggests they were key advisors but also had responsibility for protecting the queen.

4. Relations with Parliament

The image implies that the queen has power over Parliament, as the monarch is in the centre surrounded by members of the House of Lords with MPs standing. However, the image also suggests that there is a partnership between the queen and Parliament, as Parliament is required to raise taxes and pass key laws. This in turn suggests the idea of the queen in Parliament, where laws passed by Parliament strengthened Elizabeth's authority.

5. Marriage and succession

One reason why Elizabeth did not formally name an heir was because of divisions in court. These divisions became increasingly clear after the death of Lord Burghley in 1596 and led directly to the Essex rebellion of 1601. Naming an heir – possibly James VI of Scotland – would only have made these divisions worse. Courtiers would have tried either to win favour with the future monarch or to back rival claimants to the throne, such as the Earl of Derby or the Infanta of Spain. This could have led to civil war.

Naming a successor would also have weakened Elizabeth's position in relation to Parliament. Parliament had urged her to name a successor. So, for Elizabeth to do so would suggest it was Parliament and not the queen and her Privy Council who ruled England. This would have reduced Elizabeth's authority.

6. Elizabeth's authority in later years

Any **two** from:
*   As Elizabeth grew older she became more bad-tempered and less able to make effective decisions.
*   Many of her key advisors had died: Francis Walsingham in 1590, Francis Knollys in 1596 and William Cecil in 1598. This shifted power in the court and Parliament, leading to power struggles as new men, such as the Earl of Essex, tried to increase their influence.
*   Some of the new courtiers were less respectful of the queen and began challenging her authority. For example, the Earl of Essex nearly drew his sword on her, an act that would lead eventually to Essex's rebellion.
*   Elizabeth increasingly relied on Parliament for money. She called Parliament in 1593 and again in 1601 to raise taxes. This dependence on Parliament weakened her and made her more vulnerable to Parliament's demands over the succession.
*   Bad harvests throughout the 1590s led to food shortages and rising discontent in the countryside. This reduced Elizabeth's popularity and made rebellion more likely. Falling wages and increased taxation to pay for a military expedition to Ireland in 1601 did not help the situation.

7. Essex's rebellion, 1601

One reason why Essex's rebellion failed was because he lacked enough support. He overestimated the number of noblemen who would support him. Even those who were sympathetic to his case were not prepared to risk everything by challenging Elizabeth.

Another reason was that the government knew about Essex's plot, because they had spies in Essex's camp, including Ferdinando Gorges. This allowed the government to prepare for the rebellion by confining people to their houses. It also enabled them to disrupt Essex's plans as all of Essex's prisoners – whom Essex planned to hold as hostages – were released by Gorges. Without hostages to negotiate over, Essex had no choice but to hand himself over to the authorities for trial.

Life in Elizabethan times

8. Living standards and fashions

Dress and fashion were important in Elizabethan society because they established rank and social status. The Sumptuary Laws of 1574 were rules that told people what they were allowed to wear. For example, only royalty were allowed to trim their clothes with ermine. Failure to follow these rules could result in arrests, fines and even execution. The point of these laws was to encourage conformity and respect for authority.

9. Prosperity and the gentry

- There was growth in industries, such as wool, iron, tin and copper.
- London became increasingly important as a centre of finance and trade.
- Wealth was brought into the country as a result of privateering.

10. The Elizabethan theatre

Any **two** from:

- The theatre was a form of popular entertainment that was available to all classes – the nobility, gentry, merchants and the poor.
- The theatre reflected the values, habits and beliefs of Elizabethan society. These included vulgar behaviour, obsessions with witchcraft and religious debate.
- The theatre was a commercial enterprise. Actors such as Richard Burbage and playwrights such as Ben Jonson and Christopher Marlowe could make money by writing and staging plays.

11. Attitudes to the theatre

- Theatres often attracted large crowds of poorer people, so some people saw them as a threat to public order and a source of theft. People who owned property close to theatres often opposed them for this reason.
- Puritans regarded the theatre as ungodly and sinful. They argued that theatres were associated with bawdy, drunken behaviour and prostitution, and that the players were disreputable characters who would corrupt ordinary people.

12. Reasons for the increase in poverty

Population growth was important in causing poverty in Elizabethan England, as the population grew from 3 million in 1551, to 4.2 million by 1601. This increased demand for food, driving up prices while increasing the labour supply and reducing wages. However, there were other reasons for poverty, including bad harvests, economic recessions – especially caused by trade embargos involving Spain – and enclosure. The latter drove large numbers of people off the land, and they were then unable to provide for their families. This in turn created a population of 'landless labourers' and vagrants.

13. Attitudes to poverty

During Elizabeth's reign, attitudes towards the poor were initially very negative. In medieval times the Church taught that people had a Christian duty to help the poor. However, after 1500 enclosure and a growing population meant that the poor became an increasingly visible presence in Elizabethan England. This meant that Elizabethans generally saw the poor as a financial burden and not, as was the case in medieval times, deserving of charity. They resented having to pay poor rates to provide for them, as stated by the 1563 Statute of Artificers Act. Also, increased vagrancy during the Elizabethan period meant that people increasingly wanted to punish rather than help the poor. For example, the Vagabonds Act of 1572

allowed vagrants to be whipped, mutilated and even executed. However, following poor harvests in 1562, 1565, 1573, 1586 and the 1590s, government policy towards the poor changed. They adopted a more progressive attitude, in an attempt to avoid public disorder, rebellion and food riots. For example, under the 1576 Poor Relief Act, Justices of the Peace were required to provide the poor with materials that they could use to make things they could sell. People also set up charitable foundations to help the poor, such as Lady Cecil's Bequest for Poor Tradesmen, founded in Romford in 1589.

14. Government action

- The government succeeded in establishing a system of 'poor relief' to provide for those in poverty. The 1572 Vagabonds Act introduced a national poor rate, which was a way of funding poor relief by requiring all members of the parish to pay a Poor Law Tax. This ensured that the poor were provided for and did not starve. The 1601 Poor Law Act provided workhouses for the employment of the able-bodied poor and established a system that standardised the treatment of the poor in all parishes in England.
- Legislation, including the 1576 Poor Relief Act and the Poor Law Act of 1601, helped to maintain law and order by ensuring that the poor received some assistance or relief from local parishes. The rebellions and disturbances feared by many Elizabethans did not materialise, suggesting that government action was successful.

15. Hawkins and Drake

Any **two** from:

- They began an era of privateering and piracy on the western coast of the Americas – an area that had previously been free of piracy. This increased their personal wealth and that of the Crown, which was prepared to invest in these activities.
- Their activities led to the expansion of trade, especially involving West Africa and the West Indies. Here, the triangular trade offered opportunities to make profits through the sale of slaves, sugar and tobacco.
- They encouraged further exploration. For example, when Drake completed the second circumnavigation of the globe, others were encouraged to follow his example.

16. Circumnavigation, 1577–1580

- England's reputation as a naval power increased, as Drake had overcome considerable difficulties to circumnavigate the globe. This established England as a major seafaring power.
- It meant that England could begin to expand its trade into the Indian Ocean and the Pacific Ocean. This opened up trade links with China, West Africa and India.
- It led to further exploration and colonisation, especially in the New World (the Americas). Colonies were established in New England on the east coast of America in the late 16th and early 17th centuries.

17. Voyages and trade

Any **two** from:

- English traders and merchants were able to make big profits from trading with other countries. This was especially the case with the triangular trade, which offered merchants the opportunity to make profits by trading iron goods, slaves and tobacco.
- The Crown benefitted by charging taxes on imported goods. It also made money by granting trading licences to organisations such as the Barbary Company and the East India Company for the right to trade in the West Indies and the Far East.
- Trade allowed new goods, including potatoes, tobacco, coffee, spices and dried grapes, to enter English markets.

18. Sir Walter Raleigh

Raleigh encouraged exploration and colonisation of the New World by getting investors to fund expeditions to Virginia. Raleigh's attempts to establish colonies failed, but his actions led to further expeditions during James I's reign.

They also forced English governments to think about how they organised future settlements. While Raleigh had tried to pay for expeditions by raising money from friends who were prepared to invest in them, future exploration and settlement used Joint Stock Companies. Here, investors bought shares in future expeditions in return for a share in any profits that were made. This was an improvement as the companies were professionally managed and paid a share of the profits to their shareholders. This encouraged more people to invest, leading to more expeditions and settlement in the New World.

Troubles at home and abroad

19. The question of religion

Any **two** from:

- Catholics would have opposed the Act of Supremacy, as it made the queen and not the pope the Head of the Church.
- Catholics would also have opposed the Act of Uniformity and the Book of Common Prayer, as they required services to be in English; for Catholics, services should be in Latin.
- Catholics would have opposed the ending of traditional Catholic beliefs and practices including transubstantiation, pilgrimages and the celibacy of priests.

20. The Northern Rebellion

The Northern Rebellion threatened Elizabeth's position because it demonstrated the disloyalty of the queen's Catholic subjects in the north of England. The Northern Earls, Thomas Percy and Charles Neville, resented their isolation at court and the arrival of the 'new men' of lower social status such as William Cecil, all of whom were Protestant. At the same time many ordinary Catholics disliked the way Protestantism was being forced on them through Elizabeth's religious settlement. As a result they were prepared to lead a revolt that would depose Elizabeth.

This threat was increased by the presence of Mary Queen of Scots, who presented herself as an alternative – Catholic – monarch to Elizabeth. Thomas Howard, Duke of Norfolk, planned to marry Mary, who would then become queen in Elizabeth's place; Elizabeth's religious settlement would then be abolished and Catholicism restored in England. Many Catholics were prepared to support a rebellion that meant that Mary would replace Elizabeth as queen, which is why the Northern Rebellion was a real threat to Elizabeth's position as monarch in 1569.

21. Elizabeth's excommunication

One reason why Catholics were treated more harshly after the papal bull of 1570 was that, in Catholic eyes, Elizabeth's status had changed. She was no longer the legitimate ruler of England and they were therefore free to challenge, and even seek to overthrow, her. This, in the eyes of Elizabeth and her government, represented a turning point, as it increased the threat posed by Catholics. In turn, this led to an increasing series of restrictions against Catholics, including recusancy fines, the banning of the Mass, and the arrest and torture of Catholic priests.

22. Catholic plots 1

The Jesuits were severely treated because they were seen as encouraging rebellion. Elizabeth's excommunication in 1570 meant that Catholics were no longer required to accept her authority as a Protestant monarch. As a result, any attempt to convert people to Catholicism was seen as encouraging rebellion against the queen. The threat of rebellion and therefore treason against the queen meant that the Jesuits, unless they agreed to act as informers, had to be dealt with severely by executing those involved – usually by hanging, drawing and quartering. Other Catholics, including other priests and those who sheltered them, were also seen as traitors and were dealt with in the same way. Sixty-four Catholic priests were executed between 1581 and 1588. Additionally, the secretive nature of the Jesuits' behaviour, such as travelling in disguise and hiding in priest's holes, seemed to confirm the fact that they were plotting against the queen. This is reflected in the severity of the sentences they received.

23. Catholic plots 2

- Sheltering a Catholic priest was punishable by death and Catholics who refused to attend Protestant services were fined heavily.
- The government became increasingly suspicious of Catholics and tried to uncover their plots using a network of spies and informers. This meant that Catholics found themselves increasingly watched and under suspicion, even if they were not involved in plots against the queen.

24. Puritans and Puritanism

- The Puritans threatened Elizabeth's government because they challenged the religious settlement of 1559. They were prepared to discuss and approve changes to the Church's thinking without the queen's permission, which weakened her authority. For example, the Lambeth Articles of 1595 included many Puritan beliefs – these were discussed and approved within the Church without the queen's permission.
- Puritan tracts could be critical of the queen and the Church. For example, the Martin Marprelate tracts accused the queen and her government of being 'anti-Christian'. Such comments weakened the queen's authority and could encourage rebellion. As Archbishop Parker stated, Puritan ideas would 'undo the queen and all others that depended upon her'.

25. Response to religious matters

Any **two** from:

- Whitgift increased the powers of the Church Court of High Commission so he could use it to take action against Puritan clergy. For example, in 1589 the Court banned Puritan preaching in London parishes.
- Under the Court's authority, Puritan printing presses were found and closed down, making it difficult for them to spread their ideas and win support within English society.
- As a Privy Councillor, Whitgift was able to persuade Parliament to pass the Act against Seditious Sectaries of 1593 making Puritanism an offence. This prevented Puritans from distributing leaflets promoting their ideas.
- Whitgift's influence as a Privy Councillor and the increased powers given to the Church Court of High Commission meant that Puritans could be persecuted effectively. For example, both Thomas Cartwright and Peter Wentworth were imprisoned, while John Greenwood and Harry Barrowe, who both supported separation from the Church of England, were executed in 1593.

26. Mary's arrival in England

Any **two** from:

- Mary Queen of Scots' arrival posed a problem for Elizabeth because, by remaining in England, she could encourage rebellion. Many members of the Catholic nobility believed they could overthrow Elizabeth and place Mary on the throne. This was the case with both the Northern Rebellion of 1569 to 1570 and the Ridolfi plot of 1571.
- Mary believed she had a valid claim to the English throne and was prepared to participate in plots and conspiracies against Elizabeth. This was the case in the Babington plot of 1586.
- Mary's arrival in England placed Elizabeth in a difficult position. If she took action against Mary, as an anointed monarch, she would be questioning the authority of all anointed monarchs, which could encourage others to rebel against her. However, if she failed to act against Mary, Elizabeth would look weak, which in turn could encourage rebellion.

27. Mary's treatment in England

- Mary was held captive because Elizabeth had no other ways of dealing with her. If she was released, she could threaten Elizabeth's throne. If she remained in England, she could inspire Catholics to plot against the queen. If she went abroad, she could work with the French and Spanish governments to launch an invasion of England and gain the throne by force. Keeping Mary in England was therefore the best option available to Elizabeth.
- Trying and executing Mary would result in the death of an anointed monarch. This could send out a dangerous message that it was acceptable to kill an anointed monarch – and in the wrong circumstances this could result in the execution of Elizabeth herself. Elizabeth therefore decided she had to keep Mary prisoner rather than killing her.

28. Removing Mary

Elizabeth benefitted from Mary's execution because it removed an important threat to her monarchy, as there was now no alternative monarch readily available to replace her. This meant there was less opportunity for future Catholic plots against the queen.

However, the execution also threatened Elizabeth. It angered Spain and gave Philip II further reason to attack England, especially as he had been married to the prior Queen of England, Mary Tudor. Also, Mary was an anointed monarch, so executing her set a dangerous precedent: in the wrong circumstances Elizabeth could meet a similar fate. So the execution made Elizabeth and her heirs more vulnerable in the future.

29. Reasons for conflict

England's trading activity caused conflict with Spain was because it posed a threat to Spanish interests. Since the late 1400s Spain – with Portugal – had claimed the right to explore and trade with the New World. This had enabled Spain to acquire enormous wealth through gold, silver, sugar cane and tobacco. English trading activity, especially in the Far East and the New World, challenged Spain's financial superiority, increasing tension between the two countries.

30. Naval warfare: tactics and technology

- English ships, unlike those of the Spanish, had smaller cannons that could be reloaded quickly. This enabled them to cause significant damage to Spanish ships from close range. Spanish cannons were bigger but harder to reload.
- English ships, unlike Spanish ships, had full rigging. This allowed them to manoeuvre more easily among enemy ships and then sink or damage them using cannons.

31. The defeat of the Spanish Armada

English tactics were helped by English ship design, as English galleons were faster, easier to manoeuvre and contained smaller cannons that were quicker to reload. This meant that the English ships were able to get close enough to the Spanish ships to fire on them, but stayed far enough away to prevent Spanish sailors and soldiers from boarding. In this way, the English were able to destroy and damage a number of Spanish ships, killing many of their crew, while ensuring that English losses were minimal. This demoralised the Spanish and made it difficult for them to link up with the Duke of Parma's army in the Spanish Netherlands.

Another reason was Drake's use of fireships at the Battle of Gravelines. This was important as it caused the Spanish to panic, cut their anchors and drift out into the North Sea. This meant that the Armada broke up and was forced to sail around the British Isles, making it vulnerable to the stormy weather, which destroyed more than a third of the ships.

The historic environment of Elizabethan England

32. Site investigation

Answers will depend on the site studied. For example, using the sample site, Speke Hall, on pages 33 and 34:

- Location – Speke Hall is located in the north-west of England close to the Mersey Estuary.
- Function – Speke Hall was a place of residence for the Norris Family between the reigns of Henry VII and Charles II.
- Structure – Speke Hall was a wattle and daub house with a sandstone base.
- People – The people who lived in the house during Elizabeth's reign were the Norris family, who were Roman Catholic.
- Design – By 1598 the house had been designed so that an enclosed courtyard was surrounded by timber-framed buildings.
- Culture, values and fashions – The Norris family saw themselves as members of the gentry and this is reflected in their coat of arms, which suggests they were an important family.
- Important events and developments – Elizabeth's religious settlement of 1559 meant that the Norris family, as Catholics, had to alter the design of the house to avoid discovery. This involved the addition of priest's holes, eavesdrops and peepholes.

33. Sample site: Speke Hall 1

Any **two** from:

- One feature that demonstrates that the residents of Speke Hall were Catholic is a priest's hole, which allowed visiting priests to hide from the authorities.
- Another feature is a peephole, which allowed the occupants to see who was approaching the house.
- A further feature is an eavesdrop, which was a hole under the eaves to allow servants to listen, without being seen, to the conversations of guests.

34. Sample site: Speke Hall 2

Any **two** from:
- The construction of the North Range in 1598 and the extension of the South Wing between 1540 and 1570 meant that family members slept in their own rooms and enjoyed a degree of privacy. The fact the family no longer slept in the Great Hall with the servants showed their relative wealth and importance.
- The use of glass, incorporating the coat of arms of the Norris' and related families, would also advertise the family's status and wealth.
- The Norris family's status was also shown in the way they followed Tudor fashions and dress codes. As members of the gentry they could wear gilt or velvet.
- The external appearance of Speke House, with its sandstone foundation, painted exterior and timber frame, was another indication of the family's wealth and status.

35. Sample site: Blackfriars Theatre 1

The function of Blackfriars Theatre changed because of the size of the audiences watching the plays. The second Blackfriars Theatre, built in 1596, was a roofed theatre in which plays were performed for large audiences of between 600 and 1000 people. This contrasted with the original Blackfriars Theatre, which was much smaller and located in the old refectory of the Blackfriars monastery. This first theatre had only been suitable for plays shown privately to small audiences.

36. Sample site: Blackfriars Theatre 2

- The plays shown reflected the vulgar humour of Elizabethan society. For example, plays by Thomas Middleton, Ben Jonson, George Chapman and John Marston poked fun at leading figures in society, were often violent and included sexual content.
- The use of public galleries allowed the wealthier members of society to be seen by others. This reinforced their status and importance.

PRACTICE

46. Practice

13 The interpretation is convincing about the threat posed by Mary Queen of Scots because it suggests she was involved in a plot to assassinate Queen Elizabeth. Mary did offer her support in writing to Catholic plotters, including Anthony Babington, who intended to assassinate the queen. The plan was that Elizabeth's assassination would be followed by a French invasion of England led by the Duke of Guise, allowing Mary to become queen and Catholicism to be restored to England.

Mary, even while she was Elizabeth's prisoner, remained a threat to the queen and her throne, as she was prepared to plot in writing with those who wished to depose Elizabeth. Mary had been at the centre of previous plots, including the Northern Rebellion of 1569–1570, the Ridolfi plot of 1571 and the Throckmorton plot of 1583. As Elizabeth's cousin, Mary was a potential successor to her throne. She was a threat because she was Catholic, which meant that she was always central to Catholic and overseas plots that aimed to replace Protestant Queen Elizabeth with a Catholic monarch.

However, the threat posed by Mary Queen of Scots in the interpretation may be exaggerated. Elizabeth's spymaster, Francis Walsingham, was able to decipher Mary's correspondence, arrest Babington and execute the other plotters. So while Mary may, as the interpretation implies, have wanted to end Elizabeth's life and seize the throne, the actions of Elizabeth's government meant it was unlikely the plot would succeed. Also, the plot described in the interpretation was based on correspondence between Babington and Mary that suggested she was willing to have Elizabeth murdered. There were many people in Elizabeth's government and Parliament who, by 1586, wanted Mary dead. The threat posed by Mary, as suggested by this interpretation, may therefore have been exaggerated in order to bring about Mary's execution.

48. Practice

14 Puritanism posed a major problem for Elizabeth's government, as many Puritans did not accept the religious settlement of 1559. Some Puritans did not approve of the Act of Supremacy and did not think a monarch could be Head of the Church in England. Other Puritans wanted to abolish the positions of bishop and archbishop, which they saw as unnecessary. Others wanted to end the use of special clothes or vestments that were worn during church services. In these ways Puritans challenged Elizabeth's religious settlement and also the queen's authority as Head of the Church in England.

Puritans also encouraged people to criticise the government, which undermined its authority further. Religious pamphlets such as the Martin Marprelate tracts accused the queen and her ministers of being 'anti-Christian'. They were produced by Puritan printing presses and could be read by large numbers of people. Puritans also encouraged opposition in Parliament through the Puritan Choir, a group of Puritan MPs who challenged the government over issues such as the royal succession. As Archbishop Parker stated, Puritan ideas threatened to 'undo the queen and all others that depended upon her' – that is, to undermine her authority as queen and create instability.

Puritans also weakened the monarch's control of the Church of England. For example, the Lambeth Articles of 1595 setting out Church doctrine were published by the Church of England synod without consulting the queen. When Elizabeth found out she was furious and demanded they be withdrawn.

Other Puritans wanted to separate from the Church of England completely. For example, both John Greenwood and Harry Barrowe were executed for encouraging this. This again shows how the religious practices of some Puritans were beyond the control of the Elizabethan government, and how they undermined Elizabeth's monarchy and encouraged rebellion and disagreement.

50. Practice

15 The Babington plot affected Elizabethan England because it demonstrated the determination of Catholic plotters to overthrow Elizabeth. This determination is suggested by the details of the plot that Francis Walsingham and his spies discovered. Key Catholics including Thomas Babington, Philip II of Spain and the pope supported the plot. The plan was that the Duke of Guise would invade England, overthrow Elizabeth and put Mary Queen of Scots on the throne.

The discovery of the plot was significant for Elizabeth's government, as it demonstrated that neither English Catholics nor Mary Queen of Scots could be trusted. Instead, they were traitors who were determined to overthrow the monarch and restore Catholicism in England. Walsingham and William Cecil were able to use the evidence of the plot they had discovered to persuade a reluctant Elizabeth to execute Mary Queen of Scots in February 1587. Mary's execution turned her into a Catholic martyr, but it also weakened the Catholic cause in England by removing a figurehead for Catholic plotters to rally around. However, Mary's execution as an anointed monarch had consequences, as it made it easier to kill other rulers. These included Elizabeth herself and also her heirs: the assassination of James I was attempted in the Gunpowder Plot, and Charles I was executed in 1649 during the English Civil War.

In addition, Mary's execution angered Spain at a time when Philip II was already angry about English interference in the Spanish Netherlands. As a result, Mary's execution turned England's declining relations with Spain into outright war. This led directly to the attempted invasion of England by the Spanish Armada in 1588.

The Babington plot also resulted in the increased suppression of Catholics in England. The plotters, including Babington himself, were hung, drawn and quartered, with the gallows erected very high as a visible warning to others prepared to plot against the queen. In the aftermath of the plot, many Catholics who refused to attend Protestant services had to pay recusancy fines, while Catholic homes were raided and searched by Elizabethan 'priest hunters', such as Richard Topcliffe. In this way Catholics became a minority persecuted by the state and forced into financial hardship.

52. Practice

16 Answers to Question 16 should:
- balance evidence to make a clear, logical argument
- describe any aspects/features that support the statement and explain why
- describe any aspects/features that either contradict the statement or that you would expect but are missing, and explain why.
- include the seven key factors (location; function; structure; people; design; culture, values and fashions; and important events and developments)
- relate your knowledge to the site and the site to your knowledge (you need to do both)
- make a judgement about which side of the argument is stronger – this is your 'how far'.

For example, an answer to Question 16a about Elizabethan manor houses, referring to Speke Hall, might look like this: Elizabethan manor houses demonstrated the growing power and influence of the gentry, which is clear from a study of Speke Hall. They also demonstrated the growing religious divisions in Elizabethan England, at a time when Catholics were under pressure to conceal their faith.

Elizabethan manor houses reflected the gentry's wealth and power. The design of, and extensions to, Speke Hall between 1540 and 1598 allowed the Norris family more privacy. They now had their own bedrooms and neither they nor their servants had to sleep in the Great Hall – which had been a common practice during the 15th century.

The external appearance of Speke Hall, with its red sandstone foundations, courtyard and painted exterior, demonstrated the Norris family's wealth and importance and gave a sense of their status and power. This is further reinforced by Speke Hall's location close to the Mersey estuary. This location provided the house with a prominent position in the local landscape that meant it was visible to many people living in the local area.

Changes to the interior of Speke Hall also suggest the growing power and influence of the gentry, with coats of arms visible above the fireplace and on the glass in the windows. These features implied that the Norris family was a family of some importance. These points show that access to cheaper building materials had allowed the gentry to expand their houses and enhance their status.

Speke Hall also provides evidence of religious change and religious divisions in Elizabethan society. The Norris family was, like many other members of the gentry in the north of England, Roman Catholic. This meant that, by the 1580s, it was necessary for them to take steps to conceal their religion as suspicion of Catholics grew. This led to the construction of priest's holes, peepholes and eavesdrops, all of which were designed to conceal their religious practices and hide visiting priests. This was especially important after 1585, when changes in the law made the concealment of a Roman Catholic priest punishable by death. In addition, by the late 1590s, recusancy fines – for failure to attend Protestant Church of England services – were increasing. This meant that the family increasingly lacked the money to further extend the property in a major way. The extent to which the house could continue to demonstrate the power and influence of the gentry was, in the case of the Norris family, therefore quite limited.

In conclusion, Elizabethan manor houses such as Speke Hall demonstrate the growing power and influence of the gentry in Elizabethan England. However, they also – especially in north-west England – suggest the impact of religious change and persecution and the steps their owners were forced to take to conceal their religious practices from others.

Published by Pearson Education Limited, 80 Strand, London, WC2R 0RL

www.pearsonschoolsandfecolleges.co.uk

Text and illustrations © Pearson Education Ltd 2018
Typeset and illustrated by Kamae Design
Produced by Out of House Publishing
Cover illustration by Eoin Coveney

The right of Brian Dowse to be identified as author of this work has been asserted by him in accordance with the Copyright, Designs and Patents Act 1988.

First published 2018

21 20 19 18

10 9 8 7 6 5 4 3 2 1

British Library Cataloguing in Publication Data
A catalogue record for this book is available from the British Library

ISBN 978 1 292 20480 2

Printed in Slovakia by Neografia

Acknowledgements
Content written by Rob Bircher, Sally Clifford, Victoria Payne and Kirsty Taylor is included.

The author and publisher would like to thank the following individuals and organisations for permission to reproduce copyright material:

Photographs
(Key: b-bottom; c-centre; l-left; r-right; t-top)

Alamy Stock Photo: Art Collection 2, 3, 25b, World History Archive 4, 18, 21t, IanDagnall Computing 6, Falkensteinfoto 7, Christopher Nicholson 9, Granger Historical Picture Archive 11, Ian Dagnall 15t, Lebrecht Music and Arts Photo Library 15b, GL Archive 21b, Paul Fearn 25b, 30t, Ron Jones 33, The National Trust Photo Library 34b, Debu55y 34t, Science History Images 36; **Bridgeman Images:** Queen Elizabeth's Galleon (woodcut), English School, (17th century)/Private Collection 30b, Queen Elizabeth I rebuking the Earl of Essex (litho), Rainer, Paul (20th century)/Private Collection/© Look and Learn 39

All other images © Pearson Education

Text
Text on pages 1, 2, 8, 10, 12, 13, 19, 20, 22, 23, 24, 26, 27, 29 and 31 from Dowse, Brian; *Revise Edexcel GCSE (9–1) History Early Elizabethan England, 1558-88 Revision Guide and Workbook;* © 2017. Published by Pearson Education Limited, pages 1, 2, 13, 27, 28, 29, 8, 7, 15, 16, 17, 10, 13, 14, 20 and 24.

Note from the publisher
Pearson has robust editorial processes, including answer and fact checks, to ensure the accuracy of the content in this publication, and every effort is made to ensure this publication is free of errors. We are, however, only human, and occasionally errors do occur. Pearson is not liable for any misunderstandings that arise as a result of errors in this publication, but it is our priority to ensure that the content is accurate. If you spot an error, please do contact us at resourcescorrections@pearson.com so we can make sure it is corrected.